Pass It On!

Pass It On!

MICHELLE MORAN

Foreword by Jim McManus CSSR

Darton, Longman and Todd
London

First published in 1990 by
Darton, Longman and Todd Ltd
89 Lillie Road, London SW6 1UD

British Library Cataloguing in Publication Data

Moran, Michelle
  Pass it on!
  1. Catholic church. Evangelism
  I. Title
  269.2

  ISBN–0–232–51896–3

Unless otherwise stated scriptural
quotations are taken from *The
Jerusalem Bible*, published and
copyright 1966, 1967 and 1968 by
Darton, Longman
and Todd Ltd
and Doubleday & Co Inc,
and are used by permission of the
publishers

Phototypeset by Input Typesetting Ltd,
London SW19 8DR
Printed and bound in Great Britain by
Courier International Ltd, Tiptree, Essex

Dedicated with love to Tony Bartlett and fellow pilgrims at Buckden Towers, through whom I met Jesus.

Contents

Foreword

The Church, Pope Paul VI said, 'exists to evangelise'. If evangelisation is the Church's 'deepest identity' then a reluctance or an unwillingness to evangelise would betray a very dangerous 'identity crisis'. Are we willing, during this 'decade of evangelisation', to face the challenge and bring the gospel to others?

Thankfully many Christians today are not faced with an unwillingness or a reluctance to evangelise. What we are faced with is the problem of 'know how'. Where do we begin? We no longer need exhortations to do the work, but we certainly need training. And we are very short of resource material.

Michelle Moran's book provides us with excellent resource material. This book could be read for the sheer enjoyment of seeing how an enthusiastic evangelist goes about her work. But it can also serve as a training manual. All the steps are here.

The reader will be introduced to faith sharing. Faith sharing is the essential first step in evangelisation. Theology always makes a distinction between 'the faith which we believe' and 'the faith by which we believe'. The former, the faith which we believe, is expressed in dogmas, creeds, and doctrines. You can study that all your life. The latter, the faith by which we believe, is the inner light, the inner conviction which enables us to accept that Jesus Christ is our Lord and Saviour. The faith by which we believe is pure gift. When we share our faith with another we are sharing the faith by which we believe. We are introducing another person to the relationship which we have with Christ. Michelle Moran shows us how to prepare for this kind of faith sharing and she also highlights the power of sharing one's own personal faith story.

We also need to have a very clear grasp of the core message of the gospel. What do I say? How do I say it? When do I say it? Where do I say it? These are the practical questions which we have to answer. A careful study of Chapter 4, The Gospel Message, will go a long way to answer these questions.

Pass It On! will be a great help to individual Christians; and parish groups and prayer groups, which are seeking to prepare themselves for the decade of evangelisation, could not do better than to take this timely book and work with it for three to six months.

Jim McManus CSSR

Acknowledgements

I would like to thank those many people who have shared their faith, doubts and aspirations with me, and those who have supported me on my journey of faith.

Thank you to all those who have made this book possible, especially the members of the Sion Community, through whom I have learnt so much about evangelisation. I am deeply indebted to Joe O'Boyle who helped me to express my ideas in 'good English', and to Audrey Gibbs, Fr Chris and Simon for typing the script and putting up with last minute changes. I am grateful to Charles Whitehead, who initially suggested that I might write a book, and to Morag Reeve, my editor, who persuaded me to go ahead with it and constantly encouraged and supported me.

Finally a big thank you to Peter, my husband, for his love and support, and for putting up with my moods as I struggled to get the words down on paper.

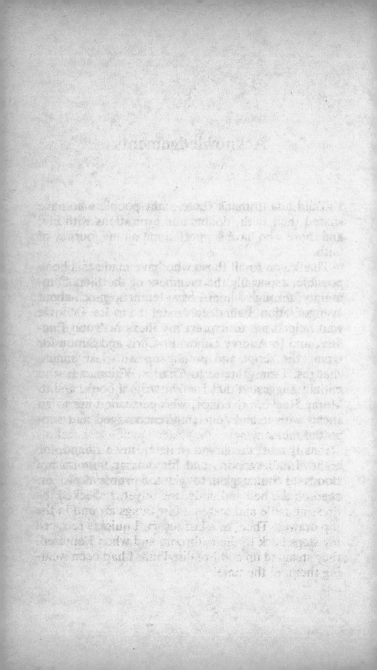

1

The Call

The harvest is rich but the labourers are few . . .
(Luke 10:2)

A few days ago I awoke in a panic, realising alas too late that it had been a mistake to turn off the alarm which had been persistently ringing almost half an hour earlier. In haste, I rushed into the bathroom and then quickly fumbled through my wardrobe, trying to find an appropriate outfit for the day. Then, the whole world seemed to be against me; the button that I had been meaning to sew on for ages, decided to fall off; my shoes suddenly seemed to cry out for polish and the slight flaw in my tights immediately turned into an enormous ladder. Meanwhile, the radio announcer calmly stated that it was just turning thirteen minutes to eight! In the midst of all this turmoil, horror of horrors, I couldn't find my glasses! Frantically I searched on the bed and under the duvet. I checked the dressing table and tossed a few things around in the top drawer. Then, as a last resort, I quickly retraced my steps back to the bathroom and when I entered, they steamed up and I realised that I had been wearing them all the time!

In the Bible, sight seems to be a recurring theme and there are several examples of people being healed of blindness. Undoubtedly all Jesus' miracles are real in a physical sense but they also convey a deeply significant underlying truth. Blindness represents unbelief and so many of the healings go far beyond the physical level because Jesus is interested in the 'whole person'.

On reflection, the rather amusing episode of my 'lost' glasses reminded me of my journey in faith which has not been so much a search to find God, but has been more of a process of discovering God who is already within me, if only I had the eyes to see. Indeed, I feel that I could constantly echo the words of Bartimaeus: 'Master, let me see' (Mark 10:51) because I am aware that so much of what we see now is merely a dim reflection of the ultimate hope we will all attain when, in the words of St Paul, 'we shall be seeing face to face' (1 Cor. 13:12).

MY STORY

I grew up in a very loving, stable family which is not particularly religious. Consequently I have very few childhood memories of God. In fact by my mid-teens I had come to quite an amicable arrangement with God, it went something like: 'You don't bother me too much and I won't bother you!' Things were going fairly well and at the age of sixteen I had just passed eight 'O' levels and was about to begin studying for four 'A' levels, whilst busily selecting a university and planning my career.

I distinctly remember walking through the newly constructed shopping precinct in Leeds, with money in my pocket to buy clothes or maybe a record, when I began to think, 'Surely there must be something more to life than this?' But I had everything, a good family, material comforts, academic success, a future . . .

Suddenly I was awakened from my daydream by the distant echo of music, heads began to turn and the busy stream of Saturday shoppers was interrupted by a lively group of brightly clad people who were making their way towards where I was standing. I was utterly mesmerised by the music which had now become clearly audible; some people were playing hand drums whilst others had bells, cymbals and tambourines. The rest danced and clapped and all sang in unison: 'Hare-Krishna, Hare-Krishna, . . .' It wasn't a particularly melodic tune but I was captivated by the colour, joy and life of the occasion. Before I knew what was happening a rather strange looking man with one long plait stopped to chat with me. At the time I was dressed in a fairly Bohemian way with my long skirt, Afghan coat and desert boots. I was therefore immediately attracted by his 'alternative appearance' and so we chatted for a while and he introduced me to some of his friends. Then I was invited for a free meal at their temple and given a complimentary ticket which also allowed me to take a friend.

As I continued with my shopping, I kept thinking about the group of people that I had met, they seemed so friendly. Unfortunately their temple was on the seedier side of town so I knew that if I was to go I would have to persuade a school friend to accompany me.

The initial visit was a disappointment; the joy and

excitement of the street encounter had somewhat faded from my memory and suddenly we found ourselves in a totally alien environment. There were strange smells, unfamiliar rituals and very unusual foods. The exciting 'alternative culture' that I thought I had discovered, had suddenly become very heavy and extremely intellectual. Many of the people spoke to us about God but it all seemed so technical and complicated and the spontaneity and joy which had so attracted me in the street had totally dissipated. In fact after a few visits we decided that the whole thing was boring, although unmistakeably something was being stirred up within me.

A few weeks later, I was invited by a group of school friends to go camping. I had never been camping before and so after hastily purchasing a sleeping bag, I boarded the minibus. As we set off down the M1, I realised that it wasn't just a camping 'holiday', it was in fact a Christian youth camp organised by the S.V.P. (St Vincent de Paul Society).

On our arrival at the camp it seemed like we were surrounded by hundreds of other young people and there was an initial air of expectancy and buzz of excitement. For most of the first day however, I walked around in bewilderment because I couldn't relate very easily to much of what was happening. Whilst it was relatively easy to side-step many of the arranged activities, in the midst of such a large crowd it was impossible to avoid the people.

During the weekend I can recall many significant conversations about God that I had with some of the young people. They seemed to have a joy deep within them and light in their eyes, and as they shared the Good News with me it began to make sense. For the first time in my life I was beginning really to glimpse the truth about God.

Over the next few months, like Mary I pondered all these things in my heart. There were some things that I didn't understand and lots of unanswered questions and although I knew that something significant was happening to me, I was frustrated because I couldn't put it into words.

Six months later, the pieces of that initial jigsaw began to fit into place. Some of the new friends whom I had met earlier in the year, prayed with me and I became consciously aware of God living within me. No longer was he a great unfathomable mystery but Jesus my friend and brother who seemed so close to me. I was given a small New Testament and on my way home, I opened it up at random and my eyes fell on the following text from Romans: 'You too must consider yourselves to be dead to sin but alive for God in Christ Jesus' (Rom. 6:11). Then I knew for certain that something momentous had happened to me, my life had been changed, not through anything that I had done but by the action of God's Holy Spirit. The seed of faith planted deep within me at my baptism had finally begun to grow and blossom. I was now living a new life!

THE CHALLENGE

In retrospect it seems incredible to think that all this happened fourteen years ago because in many ways, I am still trying to grasp the implications of being alive for God in Christ Jesus. One thing that I have learnt to my cost is that there is more to life than simply being born and that the challenge comes when we have really to embrace the demands of gospel living.

I am reminded here of the Transfiguration. It must have been such a privilege for Peter, James and John to witness that mountain-top experience, Peter displaying such a human reaction when he says: 'Master, it is wonderful for us to be here; so let us make three tents, one for you, one for Moses and one for Elijah' (Luke 9:33). There is a big temptation for each one of us to want to pitch tents and prolong the high points of our religious experience but these moments of revelation, however insignificant, are meant to strengthen and equip us for the mission of living as a Christian in the world. It is significant that when Jesus and his disciples descended the mountain, leaving behind them the experience of the beauty and radiance of God, they were immediately confronted with a boy possessed by an evil spirit. Jesus' disciples had been unable to cast it out but he 'rebuked the unclean spirit and cured the boy and gave him back to his father, and everyone was awestruck by the greatness of God' (Luke 9:43). Clearly then the power of God transforms the world and is much wider than 'personal experience'. We should therefore be prepared to descend the mountain in order to take the blinding light of God's glory into an often darkened world.

WANTED: 'LABOURERS FOR THE HARVEST'

In today's technological society there is an increasing emphasis on job specialisation and it is therefore easy to regard evangelisation as a job for the professionals, for clergy or those who have been specifically trained. But throughout the teaching of the Church we are reminded that 'evangelisation is a basic duty of the people of God' (Ad Gentes Divinitus, section 35). Notice that it doesn't say evangelisation is an optional extra in the Christian life, something that you might like to do when you feel confident or competent enough. No, it is a 'duty' and all the people of God have an important part to play in the process.

Our response to the call to evangelise should not just be because the Church asks us to but because this is what Jesus asked of his disciples. Before he ascended to the Father he conferred on them authority and told them to:

> Go, therefore, make disciples of all the nations; baptise them in the name of the Father and of the Son and of the Holy Spirit, and teach them to observe all the commands I gave you. And know that I am with you always; yes, to the end of time. (Matt. 28:18–20)

Today we are his disciples and he asks us to do the same. I am sure that many of us feel daunted by the prospects of this commission but the Lord does not ask us to go out in our own strength but to go in the certain knowledge that he is with us. Indeed we can take courage from reading the end of Mark's Gospel. First of all, Jesus reproaches them for their incredulity and obstinacy because they refused to believe those who had seen him after he had risen but he still tells them: 'Go out to the whole world; proclaim the Good News to all creation' (Mark

16:16). The Lord does not ask us to 'go' because we are holy or faith-filled people or because we have all the answers; he just simply asks us to go.

Indeed we are living in a time when 'the harvest is rich but the labourers are few'. In a traditional manner we have responded to this by praying for more vocations to the priesthood and religious life. This is important but it is also vital that we all live up to our responsibilities as the people of God. Are we prepared to be like Samuel who said: 'Here I am, Lord . . . Speak, your servant is listening'? (1 Sam. 3:4,10)

Hopefully, this book will be a source of encouragement as well as offering some practical suggestions but it is by no means a definitive work on the whole topic of evangelisation. It is, rather, a personal reflection on the practicalities of evangelism, a collection of things which I have come to see whilst working for the past five years in a community whose specific charism is evangelisation. So in Solomon's words: 'What I learned without self-interest, I *pass on* without reserve' (Wis. 7:13).

2

Lifestyle Evangelism

You will be my witnesses (Acts 1:8)

CHRISTIAN WITNESS

At the end of one of our recent evangelisation training seminars, in Exeter, a man came up to me 'grin-
ning from ear to ear'. He explained that he had
come along mainly out of a sense of duty and feeling
somewhat guilty because he knew that he should
evangelise but always felt unable to do it. He had
thought that in order to evangelise effectively you
had to be a great preacher like Billy Graham. He
returned home, however, both light of heart and full
of zeal with this myth dispelled because he could see
that the starting point was his day to day life with
those around him. His parting words were, 'I go
home conscious that my whole life should be one
which gives witness to Christ'. For many of us this
will come as no great revelation. I think what happened to the man was that something which he had
known began to take deep root in his life and challenge him.

Christian witness is indeed a powerful way of dis-
posing people to hear and respond to the Good

9

News but, needless to say, as Christians, it is our responsibility to reflect upon our own lives and make sure that we do, in fact, give a good witness. We could ask ourselves, 'Is my lifestyle and are my values any different from those of the people around me?' It is so easy to become sucked in by the world and when we do, we lose our potential to be authentic witnesses to Christ and his gospel. Many unbelievers find that Christians do not ring true because their lives are too extravagant and luxurious. I can recall one deprived inner city parish where the priest had an expensive sporty car. Now there is nothing wrong with owning a large fast car but it did seem to stand out in a locality where few people ever owned cars.

LIFESTYLE EVANGELISM

In the course of house to house visitation, during one of our parish missions, I remember speaking to one gentleman who couldn't understand why he was being visited. He went into great detail about his church involvement lest we should get the impression that he was a 'lapsed Catholic'. I explained that the purpose of the visit wasn't to check up on him but that we had simply come to meet him and that the visit was an opportunity for us to share our faith. He seemed to find our approach rather difficult to relate to and exclaimed that his faith was something private and personal and he had no intention of sharing it with anyone! To some extent I can sympathise with him because I know that, especially in the past, Catholics were not encouraged to share their faith but to regard it as a precious treasure to be personally cherished.

The Church has, however, moved on a lot since then and many people are still in the process of catching up. It is true to say that our faith is something personal because it is based first and foremost upon a personal relationship with Jesus Christ. This is the starting-point and, as such, is very significant. Many other religions, such as Buddhism, call people to adhere to specific teachings, principles and philosophies. As Christians, however, we are called primarily to a 'person', Jesus. So being a disciple means knowing him, loving him and serving him, not just in isolation but in the church and in the world.

Lifestyle evangelism involves using our existing relationships to evangelise and so as we grow in our primary relationship with Jesus we should be prepared to share his love within all our relationships. In order to do this we don't need to undergo years of theological training or develop any special skills or methods. We simply need to be open and willing to share our faith with others. This presents us with a big challenge – instead of consciously taking Christ the Redeemer of the world into our daily situations there is a big temptation to leave him at the door as we come out of church on Sunday.

Undoubtedly, the most effective place of ministry for each one of us is our daily life for we can simply reach out to that group of people with whom we relate on a regular basis. This will include members of our family, our friends, our workmates and those who live in our neighbourhood. Lifestyle evangelism is the most natural way of reaching others and, perhaps, we have lost some of the early church's zeal for communicating Christ because we have, needlessly, made things technical and complicated.

I remember, in my late teens, listening to a talk given by two missionaries about their work. One was involved in evangelism and the other in health promotion. I was very inspired by the work of the evangelist and afterwards I asked her what qualifications I would need to follow in her footsteps and I was somewhat taken aback when she said: 'you just need to allow the Good News to shine out of you and be prepared to introduce others to your friend Jesus. Don't wait until you are a missionary. Start right now with the people around you!!' In an attempt to be both practical and relevant I have selected three main areas of relationships – those in the family, workplace and neighbourhood – but, obviously, these suggestions are meant to be very general guidelines rather than hard and fast rules. Many of the observations are based upon my own experiences. However, I am aware that each person is unique and that there is a rich variety of individual situations. The two main ground rules are, simply, firstly to be open and secondly to be oneself.

THE FAMILY

The family can be the most difficult and challenging but yet rewarding environment in which to witness to Christ. Relationships exist on a variety of levels but this is the place where we are 'really known', warts and all! These are the people who are most familiar with our weaknesses, faults and problems and, regrettably, our strong points can often get overlooked or be taken for granted.

12

Obviously, we are going to know and have contact with our families for a long period of time and, therefore, there is no need to rush things. Naturally, all of us are eager for those whom we know and love to grow in faith but we must avoid, at all costs, being pushy or impatient.

I can recall many instances of people who, in moments of zeal or enthusiasm, have succeeded in 'switching off' members of their families who have simply dismissed them as religious maniacs and, unfortunately, once people have become closed to something it is then very difficult to break through the barriers.

Perhaps the key word for witnessing in the family is 'serving', that is simply loving and showing consideration for others. St Paul tells the Galatians: 'Serve one another, rather, in works of love' (Gal. 5:13).

Those who are closest to us will often notice our actions before they are ready to listen to our words. Indeed, our families are often the people who are least likely to 'listen' to us. Sometimes we might even need to change our behaviour if we perceive it to be in conflict with the gospel. After Zacchaeus had encountered the Lord so dramatically, he felt called to give half his property to the poor and pay back those whom he had cheated four-fold.

We may need to make restitution in our family situations by, perhaps, settling some long-standing dispute or by being prepared to forgive 'and' forget. Such behaviour will not go unnoticed by those around us. Recently, while leading an Evangelisation Training Seminar in Bristol, I met a lady who had returned to the church, after a considerable time, because of her nineteen-year-old son. He had become involved in a local prayer group where his faith had really come alive; so much so that he didn't leave his dirty socks and underwear all over his bedroom floor! His changed behaviour spoke loudly and prompted her to ask, 'What has come over you . . . ?'

Conversely, I have literally met hundreds of anxious parents who lament the fact that their grown-up children no longer attend church or show any outward sign of belief in God. This is often despite the fact that they were well educated in the faith and attended Catholic schools. The cry is always: 'where did we go wrong?' There are, obviously, no easy answers and each situation would have its own complexities. All that Christian parents are asked to do, however, is to ensure that solid foundations are laid so that their children's faith can grow. There does come a stage, as in all things, when they are on their own. If the foundations are laid they always have something to come back to. Indeed two members of my own family only returned to the Church when they saw that they had a responsibility to their children and this seems to be a fairly common motivation for people to be brought back into an active faith.

The only authentic way to evangelise is, however, with a loving heart. Things must not be approached out of a sense of guilt, or even duty, otherwise we may come over in a self-righteous or condemnatory manner. We do not witness so that our own consciences can be appeased but out of love for others.

Another common situation which, perhaps, requires a specific mention is that of people whose spouses do not share their belief in Christ. This can be a painful situation which, obviously, requires the utmost sensitivity and patience and one which needs to be worked at within the individual setting. St Paul says, in a very consoling way: 'The unbelieving husband is made one with the saints through his wife, and the unbelieving wife is made one with the saints through her husband' (1 Cor. 7:14).

Thus marriage partners can sanctify each other by drawing on the grace of the Sacrament. Today, this truth needs to be emphasised because many people who are married to unbelievers can so easily lose hope and be dragged down in the belief that their influence on their partner is negligible. Approaching things in a more positive way may have surprising results.

As we grow in faith, our relationship with God obviously tends to take on primary importance. It is, however, vital that unbelieving partners don't feel pushed out by this. In fact, often the opposite needs to happen. As we go deeper in our relationship with the Lord this should enrich and enhance our marriages.

My father is a very keen angler and, consequently, my mother, describing herself as a fishing widow, spends most Sundays during the fishing season alone. Similarly, I can think of many marriage partners who feel abandoned because their other halves spend so much time out of the home engaged in 'Christian activities'. I am sure that people in this situation often feel pulled in two directions but, nevertheless, a balance must be sought and, perhaps, an evening at home may speak volumes to a partner who may be feeling a little neglected.

A few days ago I met a neighbour who was very angry at the fact that her husband was again doing one of his 'acts of charity' and decorating an old man's bungalow. She exclaimed, rather fiercely, 'I've been waiting for four years to get my lounge decorated!' This was certainly one occasion where charity should have begun at home. We must present ourselves with integrity especially to those who are closest to us.

THE WORKPLACE

On average many of us spend up to forty hours per week in our places of work, so again, this is a situation which needs to be approached carefully because mistakes can so easily be made. I recall one such occasion when Ray, a friend of ours who was an ailing hippy, worked as a park-keeper in South London. He had a very dramatic conversion experience and became a Christian, as a result of which his whole lifestyle changed. He smartened up his appearance and arrived at work punctually each day.

Along with his sandwiches he carried a large Bible under his arm and during the lunch-break he would quote Scripture and deliver a mini-sermon to his workmates. They were, to say the least, unimpressed and wished that he would return to his former dope-smoking hippy days when, at least, he was easier to live with.

Sometimes, in an attempt to fit in and be accepted at work, we can, subconsciously, adopt the attitudes and behaviour of those around us. This subtle form of group pressure can be very powerful and can so easily prevent us being 'ambassadors' for Christ.

My husband worked for a while as a labourer on a building site and soon became aware that obtaining various materials for use at home was simply regarded as 'perks' of the job. He was faced with a dilemma; should he do the same and become 'one of the lads' or should he follow his own conscience and simply say 'no thank-you'? Over a period of time as a result of his example, one of the men on the site was led to remark: 'There is something different about you. What is it that makes you tick?' Thus he got an opportunity to share something about his faith and the people were receptive because he had earned their respect.

In our workplaces we are often engaged in a process of bridge-building, so helping people to see Christ at work in the world by reflecting him in our own lives. We must, therefore, live in integrity because 'we' may be the only gospel that people ever read. Jesus asks us to be 'salt to the earth and light to the world'. Perhaps if we were a bit saltier the world would be a tastier place!

THE NEIGHBOURHOOD

In the course of our married life we have lived both in the anonymity of a South London suburb and in the intimacy of a rural village community. Obviously, each environment had its own special characteristics but, generally, there were similarities in how we approached things. Most of us live busy lives and we can often become self-contained and isolated in our lifestyle and so we may then need to make a conscious effort to be friendly and open and simply spend time saying 'hello' to our neighbours.

17

During our time in London we were part of the music ministry in our parish. I remember one Sunday morning, when we were loading various instruments into the car, a neighbour, who was gardening, remarking that it was very early in the morning to be going to a concert practice. So we were able to share, briefly, with him our true destination and at the same time, issue an invitation to a special celebration that we were holding at the church.

Especially, in an increasingly secular society, we should not be afraid to identify ourselves as Christians. However, this brings with it a responsibility to be of service to those around us for no longer can we pass by on the other side of the road. Many doors can be opened by reaching out to those around us often in what seem to be small, insignificant ways.

Paula, a friend of ours, recently moved house and when her family arrived at their new home there was a card on the doorstep from the lady opposite. It contained a word of welcome to the locality and an offer of help should they require it. And on the front of the card were the words from Psalm 46: 'Be still and know that I am God'. This simple action was able to bring a moment of deep peace and blessing amid the trauma of house-moving.

Clearly we should never underestimate the value of simply being a Christian presence in a locality. Missionaries in the early church made a deliberate point of gaining whatever households they could to serve as lighthouses from which the gospel could illuminate the surrounding darkness. This encourages each one of us to let our very own Christian lights shine in powerful witness.

3

Your Faith Story

'The word of their testimony' (Rev. 12:11)

On returning to my car after a recent shopping trip, overladen as usual with groceries and other things which I hadn't intended to buy, I sat for a while catching my breath and watching children pour out of the local primary school.

Suddenly, I was gripped with a flash of nostalgia and in a moment transported back in time to my own primary school-days. Junior Six classroom with its musty smell and splintery wood floor came vividly to mind. I always hated the first part of the afternoons. The pace was much slower than in the mornings when I seemed to thrive upon the competitiveness generated by constantly practising mock 11+ papers. Usually, after lunch, I got told off either for wasting time or distracting others. The highlight of my day was, however, 3.00 p.m. when we would tidy everything away and sit on the coconut mats at the teacher's feet for 'story time'. Here I would completely forget everything else and become absorbed, totally, in the lives of the smugglers of Moonfleet or the enchanting world of Narnia. Many of the details of these stories are still unforgettably etched in my memory.

Today, I guess, most of us still find stories captivating whether they are the fictitious scenarios of the popular soap opera characters or gossip about the man down the street. We can seldom resist the attraction to get a glimpse into other people's lives and situations.

FAITH STORY

Recently, much emphasis has been placed upon the use of the 'faith story' as a means of both sharing and deepening our faith. It is easy to draw strength and encouragement from reflecting upon the lives of great saints, or even contemporary figures like Mother Teresa, but each one of us has a story to tell about the Lord at work in our lives. Some people might be able to recall a specific moment when Christ seemed to become a reality to them whilst others may remember particular instances which were significant in their faith journey.

Sandra, a friend of ours, is a youth worker in West London. Part of her work involves running a youth club on Friday evenings. As you might expect it is very difficult to insert anything spiritual into an activities based programme of table tennis, snooker, popular videos and so on.

One night she invited Dave, an ex-drug-addict, to come and speak to the young people. He simply told them his 'story' of how he had lived a life which centred around broken relationships, depression, suicidal tendencies and escapism into drugs. He then went on to say that he was almost at rock bottom when he was taken to a meeting by some friends and through listening to someone share about the power of Christ in their life knew that there was a way out of his misery.

As he spoke you could hear the sound of a pin drop. He had captured the young people's attention by simply sharing the events of his life which had led him from bondage to drugs to the freedom of knowing that he was a Son of God.

Obviously, this is a very dramatic account and may contrast sharply with the elements of your own faith story but even recalling seemingly insignificant events can help to build up our faith and that of those around us.

From time to time we visit an elderly lady and, during her frequent trips down memory lane, she often shares with us a moving story about a time when she experienced God's provision.

Apparently there was a time when she had no money and very little food left in the house to feed her rather large family. In desperation she knelt down in front of her armchair and prayed. As she stood up her hand slipped down the side of the cushion and there she found half a crown!

Faith-sharing is very powerful because it is not just conveying objective facts but it is rather the 'subjective gospel' pointing to the living God who is involved in a personal way with his people. This is perhaps why the R.C.I.A. programme, which is the official rite for bringing new members into the Catholic Church, places so much emphasis on faith-sharing. It is not enough to instruct people in the basic facts about Christianity. They also need to share in the experience of God at work in the lives of others

21

and in the community into which they seek entry. Faith is not just intellectual assent to a set of beliefs and principles, it is about allowing the power of God to come into our lives to change, transform and renew. We share, therefore, not only what we know but, also, what we have experienced, concretely, in our lives. In the words of St John:

Something which has existed since the beginning,
that we have heard,
and we have seen with our own eyes;
that we have watched
and touched with our hands:
the Word, who is life –
this is our subject.
That life was made visible:
we saw it and we are giving our testimony,
telling you of the eternal life
which was with the Father and has been made
visible to us.
What we have seen and heard
we are telling you
so that you too may be in union with us,
as we are in union
with the Father
and with his Son Jesus Christ.
We are writing this to you to make our own joy
complete.

(1 John 1:1–4)

TESTIMONY

In Revelation 12:11 (RSV) John writes: 'And they conquered him [the accuser] by the blood of the

Lamb and by the word of their testimony'. Testimony here refers to the stories of faith of the early Christians who 'testified' to the power of God in their lives through sharing episodes from their faith story.

Similarly, today, the use of testimony is very effective in evangelism. A personal testimony is simply an excerpt from our own personal story of faith. Because it is our experience it cannot be argued with although people are, obviously, free to believe or dismiss it. When we approach things from the personal angle and simply share how God is at work, in our lives, the message is conveyed in a non-confrontational manner and, therefore, people are less likely to feel threatened or back off.

Almost three years ago my community was conducting a parish mission in a rather wealthy parish in the Midlands. One evening we held a 'Gospel Night' which was not only aimed at the usual parishioners but friends, relatives and people from the locality. After welcoming people and singing a few lively songs, Ron, a member of the team, simply told his story. He spoke about when he had been a Managing Director of a large company and how his lifestyle had reflected his status. At one stage he owned not only a cabin cruiser but also a light aircraft and then one day, completely out of the blue, he was made redundant. Understandably this had a devastating effect upon him and, in turn, created havoc in his family life. Eventually he 'sank' to the level of trying to get a job as a commercial traveller with a small northern firm.

One evening, prior to a job interview, he found himself in a seedy boarding house in Bolton, Lancashire. As he sat in the rather tacky dining room, he felt that he had reached rock bottom and in his heart he simply cried out in despair and anger: 'God, if you are there, show yourself to me!' At that moment his eyes fixed upon a faded reproduction hanging on the wall of the famous Holman Hunt painting, *Christ, the Light of the World*. As he stared at the picture of Jesus standing at the door the words that he had learnt at Sunday School, in the Presbyterian Church of Scotland, gradually floated into his mind. 'Look, I am standing at the door knocking. If one of you hears me calling and opens the door, I will come in to share his meal, side by side with him' (Rev. 3:20).

Suddenly he realised that the handle of the door was on the inside and all that he had to do was open it and say: 'Lord, come into my broken life . . . I repent of trying to do things in my own strength, please take control.'

After his sharing there was no need to deliver a sermon about 'seeking first the Kingdom of God' because the people had not only been deeply moved by hearing about the faithfulness of God but they also felt challenged in their own lives. They began to see very clearly the short-sightedness of placing too much emphasis on material things which can so quickly fade away.

TYPES OF TESTIMONY

One of the most refreshing things about testimony is that each person is unique and has their own particular story to tell. Although the truth which they convey about the Lord may be similar the stories themselves are original and will, therefore, not only grab people's attention but will also hold their interest. Any experience of God becomes material for a testimony. Therefore, most people will have several testimonies which they can use depending on the circumstances.

There are several different types of testimony. Dave and Ron, obviously, have fairly dramatic stories to tell of how, when they had both reached rock bottom, albeit in very different circumstances, they called out to the Lord and he came to their rescue. This type of testimony focuses on a person's initial conversion to Jesus Christ. They would often be able to pinpoint a specific time when they invited him into their life. This would mark a significant change in their outlook and direction. They would, in effect, be 'under new management'.

Recently, whilst working with a group of young people, I had the opportunity to visit the village of Olney, in Buckinghamshire, and look around the Rectory where John Newton had once lived. We all stood in one of the upstairs rooms and sang with gusto perhaps his most famous hymn, 'Amazing Grace' the words of which, obviously, convey elements of his own faith journey. He had, apparently, been a slave trader and one night at sea, during a terrific storm, in fear and desperation he called out to God to save him. When put into context words like 'I once was lost but now I'm found, was blind but now I see' become a powerful testimony to the faithfulness and mercy of God.

Undoubtedly, there are some people, today, who could share about the experience of being 'lost and found' in their own lives and thus testify to the fact that the Lord is always close to his people but he never forces his way in, he simply waits to be asked.

Another type of testimony, which on the surface may seem less dramatic but is nonetheless valid, is the one which highlights a time when there has been a deepening in our relationship with God. I am aware that for many people, who have grown up in a Christian family, faith has been more of a gradual progression and it is often impossible to recall a specific moment of conversion.

On numerous occasions during parish missions my husband, Peter, has shared his testimony in a very powerful way. It is not a particularly dramatic story but a simple testimony of how God constantly reveals himself to us as we seek him more and more in our lives.

He tells of being a 'cradle Catholic' and there never really being a time in his life when he didn't believe in God. He did, however, have to appropriate the faith which he inherited from his parents. One significant step in this process happened during a young people's weekend at the Grail in Middlesex. On the first evening of the retreat Peter sat down next to a girl at supper and during their conversation she simply asked him: 'Do you know Jesus?' He was struck by the directness of her question and a little embarrassed by the familiar way in which she referred to Jesus. On reflection, he says that he had to answer 'yes' to her because in conscience he couldn't say 'no'. This little episode marked the beginning of his search to get to know God in a personal way just as you might get to know a friend.

In the context of an ordinary Catholic parish this type of testimony is very appropriate because it speaks to the hearts of the majority of people and prompts them to reflect upon their own relationship with God.

Clearly, we must never underestimate the power of testimony, even the simplest story can be effective because it can touch the experience of many people whose lives are not characterised by dramatic conversion experiences.

The third type of testimony is slightly different; this testifies to the work of God within a community or group rather than in an individual's life. Consequently, the way in which this type of testimony is used would be different. The emphasis here is on building up the body rather than encouraging an individual's faith. Having worked in a variety of parishes we are often able to encourage parishioners by sharing with them testimonies of other parishes.

A prayer group was established about seven years ago in the South London parish where we used to live. Although they were small in number right from the outset they saw themselves as being servants of the whole parish. Through growing together in prayer and seeking the Lord's will this small group have had a profound effect on various aspects of parish life. Today many of the thriving parish activities have their origins in ideas which grew out of the prayer group.

When elaborated a simple testimony like this can help to build up and encourage other people who feel that they are small in number and, therefore, insignificant.

Testimony is precious in God's eyes because it is a sign of faith. Obviously you have to be really convinced of something before you go around talking about it. Some people may feel self-conscious in sharing their story and worry that it might look like they are drawing attention to themselves. This can be avoided by the way in which you construct and convey your testimony. Always have in mind the reason why you are sharing which, ultimately, is to glorify the living God. He honours all our efforts and blesses even our most meagre attempts. We can draw strength from Jesus when he says: 'If anyone openly declares himself for me in the presence of men, the Son of Man will declare himself for him in the presence of God's angels' (Luke 12:8).

For many people events in their faith journey readily spring to mind as valuable material for a testimony; others may find it harder to recall specific incidents. The important thing to remember is that everybody has a testimony. It may be helpful to spend some time in prayer asking the Lord to bring to mind those moments when he has been particularly close. We often use the following exercise in our training seminars to help people reflect over their own faith journey, then it is fairly easy to select episodes which can be used as testimonies.

+ *Sense of God's presence*

BIRTH ——————————————————— PRESENT DAY

− *Sense of God's absence*

Divide the line into decades of your life and then plot and label points of God's presence above the line and times below the line when you felt he was absent, then join up the points.

Generally, in an evangelistic setting, short testimonies are the most useful. It is, therefore, a valuable exercise to prepare one or two testimonies which you feel would speak to others. You may find it useful, initially, to write them down. The basic rule is to keep things short and simple. Select one incident from your faith story and focus upon its central message because this is what you want to convey.

Just like any good story your testimony should have a beginning, a middle and an end. The beginning deals with the 'before' – basically what things were like prior to the time when you allowed the

29

Lord into the situation. It is important, however, not to over-emphasise or sensationalise the bad points, otherwise people may then only remember the negative rather than seeing the power of God at work.

The middle section should, therefore, centre directly upon the action of God. Putting religious experiences into words can be difficult but your sincerity will help to convey the message.

The final part should either, briefly, bring things up to date – this is especially important if the incident happened a long time ago since obviously you want to say that God is still at work in your life – or it should focus on the benefit of having a new outlook or changed lifestyle.

A fine example of a well constructed testimony with three distinctive sections can be found in Acts 26. When Paul is brought before King Agrippa and invited to present his defence he simple shares a testimony of his conversion from being a Pharisee to becoming a follower of Jesus. His story has so much power and conviction that Agrippa is led to say: 'A little more, and your arguments would make a Christian of me' (Acts 26:28).

PAUL'S TESTIMONY

So I beg you to listen to me patiently.

My manner of life from my youth, a life spent from the beginning among my own people and in Jerusalem, is common knowledge among the Jews. They have known me for a long time and could testify, if they would, that I followed the strictest party in our religion and lived as a Pharisee. And now it is for my hope in the promise made by God to our ancestors that I am on trial, the promise that our twelve tribes, constant in worship night and day, hope to attain. For that hope, Sire, I am actually put on trial by Jews! Why does it seem incredible to you that God should raise the dead?

As for me, I once thought it was my duty to use every means to oppose the name of Jesus the Nazarene. This I did in Jerusalem; I myself threw many of the saints into prison, acting on authority from the chief priests, and when they were sentenced to death I cast my vote against them. I often went round the synagogues inflicting penalties, trying in this way to force them to renounce their faith; my fury against them was so extreme that I even pursued them into foreign cities.

On one such expedition I was going to Damascus, armed with full power and a commission from the chief priests, and at midday as I was on my way, your Majesty, I saw a light brighter than the sun come down from heaven. It shone brilliantly round me and my fellow travellers. We all fell to the ground, and I heard a voice saying to me in Hebrew, 'Saul, Saul, why are you persecuting me? It is hard for you, kicking like this against the goad.' Then I said: 'Who are you, Lord?' and the Lord answered, 'I am Jesus, and you are persecuting me. But get up and stand on your feet, for I have appeared to you for this reason: to appoint you as my servant and as a witness of this vision in which you have seen me, and of others in which I shall appear to you. I shall deliver you from the people and from the pagans, to whom I am sending you to open their eyes, so that they may turn from darkness to light, from the dominion of Satan to God, and receive, through faith in me, forgiveness of their sins and a share in the inheritance of the sanctified.'

After that, King Agrippa, I could not disobey the heavenly vision. On the contrary I started preaching, first to the people of Damascus, then to those of Jerusalem and all the countryside of Judaea, and also to the Pagans, urging them to repent and turn to God, proving their change of heart by their deeds. This was why the Jews laid hands on me in the Temple and tried to do away with me. But I was blessed with God's help, and so I have stood firm to this day, testifying to great and small alike, saying nothing more than what the prophets and Moses himself said would happen: that the Christ was to suffer and that, as the first to rise from the dead, he was to proclaim that light now shone for our people and for the pagans too. (Acts 26:4–23)

4

The Gospel Message

For I am not ashamed of the Good News: it is the power of God saving all who have faith.

(Rom. 1:16)

Almost four years ago when we were working in a parish near Carlisle, in Cumbria, we visited a family who lived on an isolated housing estate. We had spent about half an hour talking to the wife who no longer attended church because she had, in the past, been hurt by a priest. Presently, her husband came into the room and sat down and, as we tried to bring him into the conversation, he stated that he had been a 'seeker' all his life and had found that the Buddhist philosophy seemed to make the most sense to him. Having put us on the spot he then announced that he had to go out in ten minutes and invited us to share with him briefly the central tenets of the Christian faith. We found ourselves rather apologetically spluttering out anything which readily came to mind about God, Jesus and the Church in general and as we left their home we couldn't help feeling that we had missed an opportunity to share the gospel with someone who was searching.

About six months later we were invited to take

part in an ecumenical outreach in inner London. During one of the preparatory training days we were asked to raise our hands if we weren't experienced in presenting the gospel message and leading people to Christ, and being unfamiliar with the terminology used I wasn't sure whether or not to raise my hand!

On reflection, I can see that our Catholic education and experience have given us a generally broad but uneven knowledge base. We are all very familiar with the gospel because we hear it read every time we attend Mass but few of us would feel comfortable if we were asked to share, briefly, the gospel message with others. This is perhaps one reason why we are often afraid to evangelise. So the specific aim of this chapter is to look at the central truths of the gospel and to offer practical suggestions on how to share them. But we must always remember that, ultimately, it is the Holy Spirit who is the Evangeliser: 'Do not worry about how to defend yourselves or what to say, because when the time comes, the Holy Spirit will teach you what you must say' (Luke 12:12).

Yet we have a responsibility to equip ourselves, both practically and spiritually, so that we can be used to the utmost by him.

Often in the course of our evangelisation training seminars we ask people to jot down what they consider to be the basic gospel message. After a few minutes when everyone's ideas are drawn together we usually get a list resembling the following.

God is love, the Kingdom, Jesus, the cross and resurrection, eternal life, salvation, the Holy Spirit, repentance, new life . . .

At this stage it becomes obvious that some sort of 'structure' is required in order to present the message in a logical manner. If we get the opportunity to share the gospel message with others we are not usually going to have the time to begin at Genesis and work our way through to Revelation. Nor are we going to be able to speak about every facet of the Christian faith. Therefore we need to be selective and systematic without clouding or watering down the central truth of the gospel.

THE 'CORE' GOSPEL

There are four basic truths which are integral to the gospel message. In traditional language these are: Creation, the Fall, the Incarnation and Redemption. It is obviously important to use language which can be easily understood by the average person so we would not use these actual words. We can see below how they can in fact be easily summarised.

Creation .... God's plan
The Fall..................................... Our problem
Incarnation...............................God's answer
Redemption..............................Our response

These four points become headings around which we can construct the core gospel message, they also help us to remember the material. I have found it useful to commit the main points and Scriptures to memory so that the message can be shared spontaneously and naturally.

There are a number of 'outlines' which are commonly used and they are all variations on the same theme. The following outline is the one which I feel most comfortable with and I suggest some practical hints from my own experience on how the material can be shared. The outline aims to be a springboard rather than a strait-jacket.

I have, personally, found it very helpful both in deepening my own faith and in helping me to reach out to others. So if you find it a valuable tool then use it or develop your own. The important thing to remember is that first and foremost in evangelism we must be *ourselves*. Frequently I read in books very good references which could be shared with others but often I can't imagine myself saying them. Rather than feeling guilty, in not using these, I am learning to see the value in being *myself*. And, at the end of the day, it is authenticity rather than slick talk that really speaks to people.

1. *God's plan*:

God loves us and wants us to have a full and happy life in union with him

Key scriptures:
1 John 4:8,10   'God is love . . . this is the love I mean: not our love for God, but God's love for us.'

John 10:10   'I have come so that they may have life and have it to the full.'

The truth which we seek to convey here is that God is a God of love and he wants us to experience fullness of life in him. Many people who have been brought up in a Christian tradition are very familiar with the words 'God is love' but things can remain at the level of an abstract, detached God generally loving everybody and everything. Here, however, we are trying to present the gospel in a personal way – God loves *me* completely and unconditionally. This is hard for many of us to comprehend because so much of our human love is conditional. Subconsciously, we say things like, 'I'll love you if you're good looking, or healthy, or wealthy', and so on, but God simply says: 'I love you.'

I remember sharing this message with an elderly lady, Mary, who lived in the North East. As I spoke gently to her about God's love she began to cry and amid the sobbing she said: 'How can I believe that God loves me when I can't even love myself?' It turned out that in her youth she had been a victim of incest and had, consequently, spent most of her life feeling guilty, dirty and unlovable. That day I was privileged to share with Mary the Good News about God's love and forgiveness, and for the first time she allowed God to speak his words of love into her heart as he began to heal the scars of a lifetime.

God's love is so abundant that he offers us the free gift of eternal life. For many of us, in the Catholic tradition, eternal life is something which we think about attaining in the future when we die. This is, however, only a part of the picture. Eternal life begins right *here* and *now* and lasts for all *eternity*. This is good news because many people are 'existing' rather than living. No matter how hard they try there is always a part of them which seems to be unfulfilled. Every person is made up of three essential parts, body, mind and spirit and perhaps, today, our bodies and our minds have never been so well fed, but what about our spirit, our innermost being? In the words of St Augustine: 'Our hearts are restless until they rest in thee.' There is undoubtedly much more to life than simply being born and it is this message about the *fullness* of life which we need to share with others.

2. *Our problem*:

> We are all sinners and sin separates us from God.

Key scriptures:
Rom. 3:23   'All have sinned and fall short of the
                glory of God' (RSV)
Rom. 6:23   '. . . the wage paid by sin is death;
                the gift given by God is eternal life.'

When we share this truth with people we try to help them see that we are all sinners and that sin acts as a barrier to us being in right relationship with God. This is important because if people fail to recognise that they are sinners then they have no need of a Saviour in their lives. Obviously we need to be very sensitive when presenting this material because we don't want to condemn, judge, or threaten people. This can be avoided by adopting the opposite approach to that used in the first section. Here we want to avoid being personal so it is best to speak about sin in a general way and allow them to make the connection in their own lives. We must also ensure that we don't dwell too much on the negative, always remembering that it is the 'Good News' which we are sharing.

There used to be an old man who walked up and down the Kings Road in London wearing a sandwich board. On the front it said in bold black letters: 'The wages of sin is death' and on the back it said, 'Repent for the end of the world is nigh'. I can't help feeling that he wasn't a very good advertisement for the Good News!!

From my experience of sharing this message about sin it would be true to say that the majority of people see themselves as 'good people' and they often have a problem in recognising sin at work in their lives. At the other end of the scale, however, there are people, particularly some Roman Catholics, who are all too aware of their sins and are almost bowed down with the weight of guilt and self-condemnation. Both these situations need to be handled very differently and we must never fall into the trap of automatically reciting bland formulas but instead try to speak words of life which are appropriate to the individual setting.

I can recall meeting Ray, one cold November evening, up in Nelson, Lancashire. As we stood on his doorstep and talked I was aware that very little of what we shared was actually finding a home with him. He was a successful small business man having his own tropical fish firm. He told us that he had always done the best for his family and that he was pleased now that they lived in the better part of town. It was evident that Ray had no need for God in his life; he seemed to be trusting completely in himself and finding security in material things.

When we began to talk in a very general way about sin he became quite angry and told us that he was a good man and was always willing to do a good turn for anyone. From time to time he cut his next door neighbour's lawn and he visited his elderly mother weekly. In an effort to calm him down I congratulated him for being such a good citizen and then paraphrasing St Paul (Rom. 7:15) I asked him: 'Ray, do you ever find yourself not doing the things that you know you ought to and doing the very things you hate?'

A few seconds of silence passed while he thought and then he told us about a 'shady' business deal that he had got into despite having made a vow not to get involved with one of the people who had a dubious reputation. He was led very gently to see that there were in fact areas of weakness and sin in his life.

On the whole I don't think that we got very far with Ray that evening. He didn't even invite us into his home but we certainly left him with something to think about. Who knows the ultimate effect?

3. *God's answer*:

Jesus is the way, the truth and the life.

Key scriptures:
John 1:1,14   'In the beginning was the Word: the Word was with God and the Word was God.'

'The Word was made flesh and lived
among us.'

Rom. 5:8   'Christ died for us while we were
still sinners.'

Now that we have examined the negative influence
of sin in our lives, the third stage of the gospel
presentation focuses on God's answer – Jesus Christ.
Here we seek to convey firstly who Jesus *is* and then
the significance of what he *has done* for us. It is
surprising how many people have a wrong or incom-
plete picture of Jesus. Over the years we have met
several people who merely view him as a good man
or prophet who lived 2000 years ago and, occasion-
ally, we have met people who believe him to be
some kind of astronaut!

I must say I have found it easy to explain the
incarnation by making reference to Christmas for,
indeed, very few people are unfamiliar with the story
and it can be developed by emphasising that our
faith isn't based upon an other-worldly God whom
we have to strive to reach; but it is based on a down-
to-earth God who knows what it is like to live on
earth as a person. When sharing something about
the life of Jesus it is important to pick out incidents
which are directly relevant to the situation.

When we were in Bristol, last year, I remember
chatting to a West Indian couple, Del and Everton,
and when we got around to talking about Jesus' life
I highlighted his healing ministry. Suddenly Everton,
who had been silent up to that point, asked if we
could pray with him for healing for he had been
confined to a wheelchair as the result of an industrial
accident. I don't think he would have even called

41

himself a Christian but, like so many people at the time of Jesus, he was receptive. After we had prayed there was no obvious sign of physical healing but a great weight of depression began to be lifted and Everton now refers to that afternoon as the time when Jesus gave him hope.

What Jesus did comprises the second part of this section. Again it is important to make this message personal and really speak to people's hearts about Jesus' love being so deep that he died on the cross for every one of our sins. He has paid the price and because of his death and resurrection has made it possible for us to live in relationship with our heavenly Father.

In our local prison on Thursday evenings we are involved in leading a discussion group and last Easter when we were speaking about the love of Jesus and the significance of the cross, one of the prisoners remarked that, 'Jesus must have a lot of love if he was prepared to die not just for good people but for men like us who have done some terrible things.' Little did he realise that he was actually echoing St Paul's words to the Romans: 'It is not easy to die even for a good man – though of course for someone really worthy, a man might be prepared to die – but what proves that God loves us is that Christ died for us while we were still sinners' (Rom. 5:7–9).

Then another man shared how he had become a Christian whilst being 'inside' and gradually the guilt, which at times had made him feel suicidal, was being healed. He said: 'I know that I have to serve my time because I owe it to society but Jesus has already died for my sins and forgiven me, now I've got to work at forgiving myself.'

4. *Our response*:

> Accepting God's gift of eternal life by inviting Jesus into our lives.

Key scriptures:
Rev. 3:20   'Look, I am standing at the door, knocking. If one of you hears me calling and opens the door, I will come in to share his meal, side by side with him.'
John 1:12   'But to all who did accept him he gave power to become children of God'.

All of us have been given free will and because of this we have choices to make. We can either accept or reject the free gift of God's love extended to us through Jesus or we can choose to be indifferent. Some people who have already made the initial choice may wish to respond by making a deeper commitment to accepting, continually, Christ into their daily lives through the power of the Holy Spirit. At this stage, we need to be very sensitive and discern where people are spiritually. We are not salesmen out to close a sale and so there is no need to be forceful or pushy. We must give people time to think and, if necessary, return and speak to them about it on another occasion.

If they do wish to respond, simply say a prayer with them. This is the prayer which I actually use, the first part being a summary of the gospel message and, where appropriate, I ask them to repeat the second part after me as I read it slowly line by line.

Eternal life means living forever with our loving Father. Although we are all God's sons and daughters, we are also sinners. Were it not for the life, death and resurrection of Jesus Christ we would have no hope for eternal life. Jesus Christ, both God and man, entered the world, took our sins upon himself and died on the cross for our salvation. He is risen from the dead and has made it possible for us to receive the gift of our Father's love, the gift of eternal life.

Come to me, Lord Jesus, touch me and make me whole. I know that I am weak and I have sinned. Forgive me, please, for I have offended you and hurt others. I open my heart to you, Jesus, and I ask you to help shoulder the burdens in my life.

I truly accept you as my Lord and my Saviour. I want to have a personal relationship with you.

Send your Holy Spirit at this moment to dwell deep within my heart, that I may receive your power and become a new creation. Jesus, I love you and I wish to proclaim your glory to others.

Amen.

(c) Catholic Evangelization Training School, Franciscan University of Steubenville, Ohio.

To some extent it doesn't matter 'how many' people make commitments because we are called to be faithful, not to be successful and we don't want to reduce people to statistics on our score sheet! At the end of the day we are simply servants doing no more than our duty. The rest is up to the Lord.

I'll never forget last summer when we visited some tower blocks in Hackney, East London, and got very little response because many people were too frightened to open their doors. One rather lonely lady invited us in and we talked together. After sharing some of the gospel message my rather zealous companion asked her if she would like to make a commitment and she seemed fairly open. However, I had soon realised that, in fact, she was lonely and very vulnerable and had we been selling double glazing or encyclopedias, I'm sure she would have been just as ready to say 'yes'. Clearly we need to be responsible ambassadors for Christ. We must never exploit or pressurise people.

One method of verbally presenting the gospel message has been dealt with in this chapter and I must stress that it is important to note that evangelisation isn't completed when the message of salvation has been proclaimed or when people respond by making commitments but, ultimately, when people are brought into the community of believers and are able to establish a productive, enduring and fulfilling Christian way of life.

5

Communicating the Good News

> Always have your answer ready for people who
> ask you the reason for the hope that you all have.
> (1 Pet. 3:15)

Last summer, while on holiday with my parents in
Dorset, we encountered a street preacher in one of
the busier seaside towns. He spoke rapidly with deep
emotion in his voice which was amplified by a somewhat distorted megaphone. He told us of how he
had, for many years, been a heavy drinker and wom-
aniser before being 'saved' and 'washed in the blood
of the Lamb'. At this point he broke into a rendition
of 'The Old Rugged Cross' and was, eventually,
accompanied by a bunch of drunken youths who had
just tumbled out of a local beer cellar. I carefully
observed people's reactions: the majority, whilst
obviously recognising that something was going on,
simply passed by. Some stopped for a short while
and then moved on seemingly unaffected and a min-
ority even joined in with the youths and generally
made fun of the well-intentioned preacher.

When I was a student I used to have on my wall
a Snoopy poster which read: 'When I had finally
found the answer, I'd forgotten the question!' and,

sometimes in Christianity, we seem to spend time searching for answers to questions which nobody is asking and failing specifically to meet people's needs. The majority of people were really indifferent to the preacher because he didn't seem to be saying anything which had any relevance to them and the few who did stop had difficulty understanding the message so heavily laden with religious jargon and imagery. Consequently, the door was left wide open for him to become an object of scorn and ridicule.

As we seek to share the Good News we should try to speak in ways which are relevant to people's situations. Somehow, we need to generate an interest in what we have to say, otherwise the message will fall upon deaf ears. Jesus often aroused people's curiosity before he imparted important information to them. This can be seen in his encounter with Nicodemus, where Jesus made a leading statement about the necessity of being born from above which caused Nicodemus to ask rather inquisitively: 'How can a grown man be born? Can he go back into his mother's womb and be born again?' (John 3:4–5) It was only then, when Nicodemus was open and receptive, that Jesus responded by sharing the Good News of salvation.

Similarly, when Jesus met the Samaritan woman, he evoked her interest by going against the social norms of the time and asking for a drink. Surprised by his unorthodox approach, she exclaimed: 'What? You are a Jew and you ask me, a Samaritan, for a drink?' (John 4:9) Gradually, as her interest was aroused, they entered into dialogue which, eventually, resulted in her acceptance of Christ as the Messiah.

Once we have emphasised the importance of beginning where people are the difficulty which we are then faced with is that of moving the conversation on in a natural manner towards Christ without turning the listener off or getting into irrelevant 'religious discussions'. I have found it useful to develop a few 'bridge sentences' which help to change the direction of the conversation from the secular to the spiritual. Here I can only offer some suggestions which have been of use to me but, in order to avoid sounding artificial, it would be important to construct your own bridge sentences and to think about situations where it might be appropriate to use them.

As we get to know people, on a personal basis, they usually begin to confide in us about their burdens, longings, aspirations and frustrations. If we have had similar experiences we might be able to say something like: 'You know I used to feel like that until I had an experience that completely changed my outlook on life. Would you like me to tell you about it?' It is good to ask people's permission to share things and then they are always free to say 'no'.

One lunch-time, in a school where I worked, a particular moral issue was being hotly debated and I was dragged into the conversation to give the 'religious viewpoint'. When all the furore had died down I turned to the teacher sitting next to me and said rather nervously: 'Have I ever shared with you how I got interested in spiritual things?' To my surprise she seemed remarkably open and as I spoke she listened attentively. At this point I became aware that other people in the staff room were eavesdropping. This made me feel rather embarrassed because I thought that I might be labelled as a 'religious maniac' but, on the contrary, it seemed as if people respected me for having the courage to share in this way.

Sometimes regrettably, it is much more comfortable for us to leave the conversation on a social level in the hope that our lifestyle will communicate to people but we can then miss valuable opportunities to speak words of hope into people's lives.

St Paul, in his letter to the Colossians, summarised much of what I have been trying to say in this section: 'Be tactful with those who are not Christians and be sure you make the best use of your time with them. Talk to them agreeably and with a flavour of wit, and try to fit your answers to the needs of each one' (4:5–6).

THE COMMUNICATION PROCESS

St Peter tells us in his first letter to: 'Always have your answer ready for people who ask you the reason for the hope that you all have' (1 Pet. 3:15). Understandably we often focus upon words and worry about what to say to people but we can get side-tracked into merely thinking up answers for every situation in which we might find ourselves. Evangelism is much wider than this – it is also about 'communicating' the Good News.

In recent years much research has been done into the communication process and some experts tell us that only seven per cent of the message is transmitted through words; thirty-eight per cent is conveyed by our tone of voice and a staggering fifty-five per cent by our 'body-language'.

A couple of weeks ago, we were helping to run a young people's weekend down in Essex. On the Sunday morning, Jeremy, one of the team, gave a talk about the Holy Spirit. The actual content of this was rather disappointing because the points were a little disjointed and there didn't seem to be a logical progression of ideas. The actual session, however, went very well because Jeremy is an excellent communicator. He spoke in a natural way with sincerity and conviction using illustrations which the young people could easily relate to and, in order to avoid simply talking 'at' them, he went to great lengths to draw them into what he had to say. He didn't just stand in front of the group but moved around and, at one stage, he even broke into a spontaneous drama sketch which was very amusing.

Clearly it can be seen that communication involves much more than imparting information but it is rather a complex two-way process, transcending the level of the spoken word. Perhaps underlying all that we have to 'say' to people we should also try to convey two essential things; *love* and *acceptance* and if these are missing, then we will be seriously failing in our task of communicating the Good News. St Paul reminded the Corinthians: 'If I have all the eloquence of men or of angels, but speak without love, I am simply a gong booming or a cymbal clashing' (13:1).

As a teenager I remember being taken to see the film *The Cross and the Switchblade*. It spoke to me powerfully, and I began to see the possibility of what God might be able to do in my own life. Unfortunately, the event was marred by a young man approaching me during the coffee break and saying in a schmaltzy voice: 'Do you know that God loves you and has a plan for your life?' He then smiled, artificially, baring his perfectly white teeth! My whole being reacted negatively to him and I felt like saying, 'No, but what I do know is that I don't like you!' Instead I said rather aggressively as I walked away, 'I have no desire to discuss that at the moment thank-you'.

The gospel of love can only be authentically conveyed in a spirit of love. In order to do this we need to take time, initially, to get to know people and then in love we can speak to their needs.

When the rich young man approached Jesus and asked: 'What must I do to inherit eternal life?' (Mark 10:17) he wasn't given the answer straight away. Instead Jesus entered into dialogue with him by first speaking about the Commandments with which the young man was very familiar. The young man then replied: 'Master, I have kept all these from my earliest days.' Then 'Jesus looked steadily at him and loved him'. Note how it is his eyes rather than his words which convey the love. Jesus then goes on to challenge the man but this is done in a spirit of love rather than one of confrontation.

To be accepted is another basic need which we all have. In the Scriptures we can find many examples where Jesus met people, loved and accepted them and then spoke life-giving words into their particular situations. So if we fail to communicate our love and acceptance of people then they will never really understand our message.

A few years ago when we were leading a parish

mission, in Bristol, a friend and I visited Mandy, a young single parent who lived in the St Paul's district. As we chatted together and played with her three children, she kept telling me how she really admired the work which we were doing. Eventually, she blurted out, 'You see I'm not good enough to be a Christian.' Then she went on to talk about her life which was characterised by a tangled web of relationships. Thankfully, we were able to help lift the great burden of guilt and self-condemnation from her shoulders when we told her that, 'You don't have to be good to be a Christian.' My friend brought a smile to her face and joy to her eyes when he exclaimed at the end of the evening, 'Heaven will be full of people who go around saying, "We shouldn't be here!" '

Now let us look at the following section which examines three main components in the communication process and offers some practical help as to how we might be more effective communicators.

LISTENING

I think it was George Bernard Shaw who said about some social function which he had attended: 'The only time that I wasn't bored was when I was speaking.' I expect that all of us are guilty of speaking too much at certain times. This can be a particular danger when we have got something of importance to share with people but perhaps if we took time really to listen we wouldn't have to use so many words. Peter, my husband, is by nature a fairly quiet person but he is often able to say in a few sentences what I would take about half an hour to convey.

This is partly because he is attentive to situations and really listens to what people are saying and, consequently, his words easily find a home within people's hearts.

St James offers the following sound advice to his brothers: 'Be quick to listen but slow to speak and slow to rouse your temper' (Jas. 1:19).

The great skill in listening is to be able to listen actively. Rather than just sitting back passively and allowing people to have their say we should demonstrate through the use of appropriate gestures and facial expressions that we are indeed listening. Several members of my community are involved in counselling and they always remark that listening to people is exhausting because it involves such deep concentration. We need to be both alert and attentive trying to remember anything which may be of significance. Tom, a member of the community, is especially good at remembering important details which, incidentally, he brings into conversations enabling him to develop a more intimate rapport with people and to establish friendships quickly.

We should also be alert to people's emotions and listen to what 'isn't' being said because these things can then help us to centre upon the aspects of the Good News which are going to be most appropriate to the individual.

BODY LANGUAGE

This is often referred to as non-verbal communication and includes such things as facial expressions, mannerisms, dress and posture, all of which can transmit a powerful message.

When speaking to people we should try to adopt a natural and open body posture because even seemingly insignificant things like folding one's arms can create a barrier. In the course of parish visiting we have developed a whole host of skills which aid the communication process ranging from taking care with the type of clothes which we wear so that they do not become a distraction or create the wrong impression, to ensuring that when we sit in people's homes we choose a seat which enables us to face people and, therefore, maintain good eye contact with them.

As we have already seen in Jesus' encounter with the rich young man our eyes are very important vehicles of communication. As far as possible, without staring, we should try to look directly at people when we speak to them for if we look away or down at the floor this can seriously hamper the flow of communication by creating an impression of disinterest.

As well as being aware of our own body language, we obviously need to be reading other people's nonverbal communication. Here again the eyes are very important. Jesus tells us: 'The lamp of the body is the eye. It follows that if your eye is sound, your whole body will be filled with light. But if your eye is diseased, your whole body will be all darkness' (Matt. 6:22–3).

We can often gain an insight into people just by looking at their eyes. Over the years we have met many people who were experiencing things like depression, bereavement, addiction and so on. This is often physically displayed in the dullness or emptiness of their eyes, and so we can sometimes receive an indication about a person's life, without ever a word being spoken.

SPEAKING

I am sure that the majority of us have experienced members of religious sects who come around knocking at our doors. Usually they have a prescribed text and nothing is going to make them deviate from it. On numerous occasions I have attempted to enter into conversation with them but usually after about ten minutes it becomes obvious that I am wasting my time.

We must also take steps to ensure that we don't end up just speaking 'at' people, but we should rather try to enter into dialogue with them and be prepared to listen actively to what they have to say. If people seem reticent to speak we can often draw them into conversation by asking a simple open-ended question. I usually ask something like: 'How do you feel about God?' This is purposely subjective and related to the emotions, and aims at side-stepping a lot of abstract talk about religion which can often be a side-track.

One of the most obvious characteristics which I have inherited from my birthplace, Leeds, is a rather strong Yorkshire accent (or so people tell me!). I therefore try to speak slowly because I am aware that some people may find it a little difficult initially to understand me. Generally it is important when we are sharing with others not to rush through things and therefore present a garbled message but rather we should try to remain relaxed and allow things to flow at a natural steady pace.

The actual tone of our voice also conveys a message. This is apparent if you listen to a news bulletin where the more serious items of news are usually imparted in a sober, unemotional tone, contrasting sharply with a sports commentator's voice often hoarse with excitement.

In our training seminars I usually exaggerate this point for effect by telling people: 'If you are sharing with someone about the most beautiful, joyous moment of your life then don't look and sound as though you are delivering a funeral homily!!'

On the whole in an attempt to be natural, I try to keep the 'tone' of conversations light but by that I do not mean superficial. At all costs however, we must avoid sounding heavy, dull or overbearing, always remembering that it is the 'Good News' which we are sharing. We should also avoid arguments which in my experience only occur when the conversation has moved from the level of faith-sharing to that of religious discussion. We need to be aware of this and either try to steer the conversation back on course or simply refuse to get embroiled in a 'religious debate', which can sometimes do more harm than good and here St Paul offers us some very sound advice: 'A servant of the Lord is not to engage in quarrels, but has to be kind to everyone, a good teacher and patient. He has to be gentle when he corrects people who dispute what he says' (2 Tim. 2:24–5).

6

Into Discipleship

Follow me and I will make you into fishers of
men.   (Mark 1:18)

A few months ago, I visited some friends over in
Northampton. As usual I left home later than I had
intended, so as I raced along the back roads, I hardly
glimpsed the autumnal countryside. But when I
approached Northampton and turned off the main
ring road, I passed a modern out-of-town shopping
complex where my attention was immediately drawn
to a large flashing neon sign which read, 'Drive-thru
– Fast Food'. This caused me to reflect momentarily
upon the fast pace of life which is so characteristic
of our modern society.

Indeed one of the most important factors govern-
ing our daily activities seems to be 'speed'. There is
a constant search for faster, more efficient forms of
transport and a cursory glance around any supermar-
ket will reveal numerous brands of 'instant' coffee
and soup, 'quick' oat breakfast cereals and 'fast'
stain-removing detergents. Also in recent years we
have seen the development of numerous fast food
chains and services such as Kwik-Fit exhausts, same
day dry cleaning and Fast Foto laboratories.

Undeniably this emphasis on speed and time has also had an effect upon Christianity. Many ministers are concerned about the length of their Sunday services and are careful not to hold too many weekly church activities because they know that people's time is limited. However if we look at the life of Jesus, we will see that he invested much of his time in the formation of his disciples. When Jesus called his first disciples he said: 'Follow me and I will make you into fishers of men' (Mark 1:18). And when they made the decision to follow him they entered into a process of discipleship whereby they worked alongside Jesus and were instructed by him.

Today there is a tendency to think of 'instant Christianity', but clearly disciples are made not born and evangelisation isn't completed when a person has made a commitment to Christ or indeed when someone becomes a member of a church. In many ways this is only the beginning because there is a sense in which we are all constantly in need of on-going evangelisation. St Paul sums up the ultimate goal of evangelisation when he tells the Colossians: 'Him we proclaim, warning every man and teaching every man in all wisdom, that we may present every man mature in Christ' (1:28 RSV). Discipleship is therefore a process of becoming mature in Christ and helping other people to do the same.

I think we have sometimes regrettably settled for second-best when it comes to being followers of Christ. Perhaps we have too often just concentrated upon bringing people into the church rather than forming active disciples of Christ who would in turn then reach out to others. The word disciple literally means 'to be a follower of a teacher or school'. In rabbinical circles at the time of Jesus a disciple would choose his own master and enrol in his school but Jesus completely changed that structure by calling the twelve himself. We too have been chosen, as St John reminds us: 'You did not choose me, no I chose you; and I commissioned you to go out and to bear fruit, fruit that will last . . .' (John 15:16). And we therefore also have a responsibility to bear lasting fruit.

It is not enough to plant a seed or even a shrub because in order to ensure that it bears fruit it will need to be firmly rooted, pruned and fertilised. In many secular jobs there would naturally be times of in-service training, instruction and evaluation and this is actually how Jesus trained the twelve. He gathered them together and gave them power and authority, he then sent them out with direct and explicit instructions to 'take nothing for the journey: neither staff, nor haversack, nor bread, nor money; and let none of you take a spare tunic' (Luke 9:3).

When they returned, 'the apostles gave him an account of all they had done. Then he took them with him and withdrew to a town called Bethsaida where they could be by themselves' (Luke 9:10). Clearly Jesus wanted this time to be one of evaluation and reflection but unfortunately in this instance the crowds followed them and so they ended up ministering to their needs.

Surely as responsible disciples today, we too have a duty to ensure that we create opportunities so that we can grow in knowledge, understanding and experience and reflect upon what it means to be a disciple.

THE KINGDOM AND THE CHURCH

On a number of occasions over the last couple of years I have been very privileged to work alongside Christians of other denominations and through our meeting, sharing and learning together we realise that there is so much potential for mutual enrichment. I have come to the opinion that this is a major way for ecumenism actually to occur.

It is sometimes said that we Roman Catholics have rather a ghetto mentality when it comes to evangelism and that we often interpret it merely as reaching out to those who are lapsed, alienated or on the fringes of the church. This is perhaps because we tend to see things too much in terms of church membership rather than in terms of the Kingdom. When Jesus evangelised he announced the Kingdom and apart from the memorable incident with Peter where he said: 'You are Peter and on this rock I will build my Church' (Matt. 16:18) Jesus never used the word church.

After John's arrest when Jesus went into Galilee he proclaimed: 'The time has come and the kingdom of God is close at hand. Repent, and believe the Good News' (Mark 1:15). We therefore primarily evangelise people into the Kingdom but this is usually expressed through membership of a local church. There are many people today who mainly due to infant baptism are technically members of the Roman Catholic Church but who rarely participate in its life. In our evangelistic efforts it is prudent initially to reach out to them because the land will probably be more fertile than that in completely unknown territory. However we cannot ignore the great commission to 'Go out to the whole world; proclaim the Good News to all creation' (Mark 16:16).

THE RENEWED COMMUNITY

During our parish missions one question which we are inevitably asked is: 'How many people have come back to the Church?' Understandably parishioners are keen to see church growth but the question sometimes betrays an underlying assumption that the parish mission is primarily for the lapsed and that those who regularly attend church are okay. Whilst Sion Community does seek to reach out to the unchurched and the lapsed, we also desire to help, deepen and renew the faith and life of the local parish. This is vital because there is no such thing as solo Christianity and evangelism cannot take place in a vacuum.

Jesus did not only redeem individuals, although this is crucial but he also sought to incorporate them into a transformed community. When we evangelise we must always have in our minds the community into which we want to invite people. Obviously this places a tremendous amount of responsibility upon the local parish because it must be a community that is growing, deepening and moving forward in the power of the Holy Spirit. Otherwise when we do reach out to the lapsed we will be asking them to return to the same community which they had previously left, and if we evangelise unchurched people we will not want to invite them into a stagnant parish community but one where they will be made welcome and be given help to grow in their faith.

WELCOMING THE STRANGER

One of the advantages of our constantly travelling around the country is that it enables us to gain experience of many parishes at grassroots level. On numerous occasions we have observed people's reactions to there being new faces in the congregation. The paradox is that whilst most people would readily agree to new members joining their parish I am sorry to say that in practice many of our parishes seem cold, unfriendly and exclusive.

In some cases the church seems to have become like a cosy club where everyone feels secure and in control. Then the intrusion of new people poses a threat to the established order of things. This contrasts sharply with the early church which was so vibrant and outward looking that it seemed to have a magnetic effect upon people who were attracted not only by the faith of the early Christians but also by the authenticity of their community life. In the Acts of the Apostles we read that: 'They went as a body to the Temple every day but met in their houses for the breaking of bread; they shared their food gladly and generously; they praised God and were looked up to by everyone. Day by day the Lord added to their community those destined to be saved' (Acts 2:46–7).

I have come to appreciate what a big step it is for people to return to the church or indeed to attend church for the first time. The difficulty is that we are

62

asking them to step into a foreign environment on the assumption that they will feel completely at home but in reality they may experience bewilderment simply because they are not used to the normal structure of things.

This reminds me of my first day in teaching. When I arrived at school, I parked my car in the only vacant space in the car park only to be told to my great embarrassment that it was in fact the headteacher's space! And because I arrived in the staff room early, I made a cup of coffee, then somebody mentioned very politely that in order to assist the cleaners there was an informal rule that no hot drinks would be made until break-time. During that first morning, I watched people rushing around efficiently, organising various things and I wondered guiltily what if anything I should be doing.

Unfortunately because our parishes are so large it is not always possible to identify new people and make them feel welcome. It is however encouraging to see that some parishes are now establishing 'greeters' or 'welcomers' who stand at the back and perhaps hand out hymn books but their main role is simply to say 'hello' to people and make them feel welcome.

It is however important to maintain a balance between welcoming people and being too intrusive. We need to be especially sensitive to those people who have been lapsed from the church, they need to be made welcome but they do not want to be interrogated.

I accompanied Bill to Mass one Sunday when we were working up in Leicestershire. He was a local policeman and had been lapsed from the church for many years mainly due to family traumas. Being a public figure he was obviously well known within the local community. As we stepped into the church porch, a well intentioned old lady insisted upon chatting with us in a loud voice but unfortunately her comments were less than helpful. Firstly she asked him rather inquisitively how many years it was since he had been to church and then to my embarrassment she began to ask other probing questions about his family life. Clearly we should be an open and welcoming community and one which accepts people unreservedly rather than making them feel threatened or intimidated.

When new people seek to join our church or lapsed members desire to return, this is in response to the Holy Spirit at work within them but their faith, enthusiasm and zeal can easily be dashed by regular church members who may feel uncomfortable about the occurrence of radical changes or sudden conversion experiences.

This was epitomised in a conversation which I recently overheard between two ladies who were cleaning the church. They were referring to a man who following the death of his wife had become a Catholic. They generally agreed that he wasn't coping very well since the bereavement because it had made him 'all religious' and they accounted for his daily presence at church by saying that he must be extremely lonely! Coincidentally, a few days previously, I had actually visited the man in his home and he had shared with me about a profound religious experience where he had felt the presence of the Lord very powerfully. This had occurred on the evening of his wife's death. She had been a

Catholic all her life but he was originally from a Presbyterian background and consequently he told me about the pain and anguish which he had initially been through when he felt led to join the 'Roman' church. It seemed such a pity that he had been unable to share his deeply moving faith story with anyone in his church and that some of them had simply diagnosed him as suffering from a 'bereavement induced' religious mania.

INITIATION INTO THE COMMUNITY

It is because of such instances that I heartily welcome the R.C.I.A. programme which is now being introduced into many of our parishes. Vatican II recognised that the church had become in many aspects very individualistic and it therefore sought to redress this balance by once again emphasising the importance of the church as 'community', the Body of Christ as St Paul says: 'Now you together are Christ's body' (1 Cor. 12:27).

Until fairly recently anyone who wished to become a member of the Catholic Church would initially visit the priest and then receive 'instructions' from him before being formally initiated into the community. However in our large parishes often nobody but the priest or perhaps a sponsor and the immediate family knew about or cared for these new members. In 1972 official permission was granted for the introduction of the Rite of Christian Initiation of Adults (R.C.I.A.) and this is now the official process by which people are introduced to and integrated into the Catholic Church. It calls upon the support of the whole community and potential new members no longer remain anonymous. Just like any new thing there have been some teething problems with the introduction of R.C.I.A. and in some cases it is still not being used correctly but hopefully in time it will be commonplace in all our parishes.

Last year whilst working in St Gregory's Parish, Market Bosworth, Warwickshire, I experienced with great joy the 'Rite of Election', the stage in the initiation process where the candidates are officially presented to the assembled Christian community. Each of the sponsors said a few words about their particular candidate's journey of faith and what had led them to seek entry into the Catholic Church. The testimonies not only showed how the Lord had been at work in the lives of the individuals but also how he had been at work in the parish community. It was a precious faith building experience for all of us present and one which I will not easily forget.

The R.C.I.A. process does not end once a person is baptised into the community because there is then a period of nurturing called 'mystagogia' (learning more about the mysteries of our faith) where the community and the new members move forward together by meditating upon the Scriptures, being fed in the Eucharist and performing works of charity.

If we simply welcome new Christians into our community and leave them to fend for themselves they will not be able to grow because this is like expecting a new-born baby to make its own way in the world. Thankfully the R.C.I.A. helps to integrate them into the community which is vital although they will also need to be given help with things like spiritual survival and growth. This can be an area where we are particularly weak because as we have already indicated we can sometimes be complacent about our own spiritual condition and not really want to progress more deeply, and so understandably we are at a loss when it comes to helping others grow in their faith. If this is taken to its logical conclusion, we end up with an immature infant church, perhaps this being what the writer of the letter to the Hebrews was alluding to when he said: 'Really, when you should by this time have become masters, you need someone to teach you all over again the elementary principles of interpreting God's oracles; you have gone back to needing milk, and not solid food' (Heb. 5:12).

The unforgettable words of a vicar addressing a group of young people when he said: 'Being a Christian is like riding a bicycle. The only problem is if you stop peddling you will eventually fall off!' are still ringing in my ears. In our lives we can never stand still, chronologically next year we will all be older and there is nothing which we can do about it. Similarly in our Christian life, not to go forwards is to go backwards and growth can only take place when we keep Christ central in our lives. 'I am the vine, you are the branches. Whoever remains in me, with me in him, bears fruit in plenty; for cut off from me you can do nothing' (John 15:5). We need to ensure that we are both rooted in Christ and growing in him. This comes about mainly through prayer and studying the Scriptures, our reception of the sacraments in the community of the church and our service of Christ in the world. The challenge for us is to continue to grow in each of these key areas and to assist other people in their growth in holiness.

7

Mission Territory

Look at the fields; already they are white, ready
for harvest!   (John 4:35)

In 1984 one of our closest friends Chris was ordained
into the Claretian Missionaries by a Mexican-born
bishop, in what turned out to be a very colourful
celebration. The actual service took place outdoors
in the grounds of the historic fifteenth-century
Buckden Towers, which was formerly among other
things a residence of the Bishops of Lincoln. Shortly
after ordination Fr Chris was sent to Guatemala as
a missionary and over the past six years we have
very much enjoyed reading his letters and seeing him
during his occasional visits home. It is as if we have
become personally acquainted with the spirit of Central America and in particular with the culture of the
Qu'equchi' Indians with whom he has been working.

Five years ago my husband Peter and I took the
rather drastic step of giving up our secular jobs and
selling our South London home in response to a call
by the Lord to follow him by working full-time
within Sion Community for Evangelism. Since we
were founder members of the community, many of
the finer details of our role and job description were

unable to be filled in and so for convenience we decided to call ourselves 'missionary workers'. However as soon as anyone hears the word mission, they seem to think immediately of foreign lands and so it raised quite a few eyebrows when we were asked where we were going and we gave replies like Nottingham, Leicester and Newcastle!

The word mission means 'to be sent out to perform a special duty' and each one of us has a duty to evangelise. Obviously we can't all pack up and move out to third world countries even if that were desirable but this shouldn't take away our 'cutting edge' as people called to proclaim the Good News of salvation. Although it is true that Jesus was sent into the whole world to bring the Good News to all people and nations, he nevertheless belonged to a particular country with its own history, religion and culture.

I am firmly convinced that today we are living in a missionary country. Whilst in many parts of the world there are 'not yet Christians', here in the UK we are progressing towards 'no longer Christians', no longer practising or no longer believing. Gospel values are being eroded or eliminated from our social, legal and political systems and in recent years we have also seen an increase in the number of people getting involved in various aspects of the occult, ranging from astrology to Satanism.

Perhaps this is why Pope John Paul II has called for a decade of 'new Christian evangelisation' beginning in 1990 and leading up to the year 2000, the overall aim being that when we celebrate the 2000th anniversary of the incarnation, there will be at least more of the world's population professing belief in

Jesus than do not. In our context we are asked to focus upon the re-evangelisation of Europe. Clearly the Church needs to exercise her full prophetic ministry by responding to the signs of the times and each one of us has an important part to play in this process.

St John records an incident where Jesus himself encouraged the disciples to be alert to the opportunities which surrounded them: 'Look around you, look at the fields; already they are white, ready for harvest! Already the reaper is being paid his wages, already he is bringing in the grain for eternal life, thus sower and reaper rejoice together' (John 4:35–6). Here Jesus identifies various stages in the evangelisation process, highlighting sowing and reaping. We also need to be aware of these in our own lives because evangelisation is not a haphazard process.

One of the members of Sion Community, Pat, is a retired civil servant and initially when we were trying to develop our vision for evangelism, he would constantly place before us the need to have our aims, objectives, methods and strategy clearly worked out. I have eventually come to value this as an efficient way of working because we can easily get side-tracked or go off at tangents, simply because we are not clear about our aims. It seems to me that there are three initial stages in evangelism: (a) pre-evangelisation, (b) sowing and watering, (c) harvesting and reaping. Perhaps if we were clear about our aims our work would bear more fruit.

In our increasingly secular society many people do not know the Lord in any shape or form and consequently do not even consciously recognise the need for him in their lives. It is therefore almost futile for us to start spouting the gospel message to them and undoubtedly this will fail to have an impact upon them because of their hardness of heart. In the words of the prophets: 'they have eyes and do not see, they have ears and do not hear!' (Jer. 5:21). Seeds cannot be planted in hard frozen ground and so somehow we need to break ground and help people to be disposed to the Good News. We have already examined how Jesus did this, he met people where they were and spoke to them using familiar words and concepts and so he spoke to fishermen about fishing, the woman at the well about water and the Pharisees about the law.

As we have already seen in chapter 2 we initially evangelise by being alongside people and gaining their trust, friendship and confidence. This may seem insignificant but we have to prepare the ground before we can sow the seeds.

SOWING AND WATERING

At home in Buckden, we have a small garden which thankfully almost looks after itself but last Spring I decided to be rather adventurous and I attempted to grow some vegetables. I bought a selection of seeds and sowed them as instructed in seed trays but being a novice I didn't realise that you were not supposed to put all the seeds into one small tray. As they began to grow there were too many small plants competing for light and space and eventually the plastic seed tray split apart. This incident caused me to reflect upon seed sowing and to realise that generally it is not a haphazard business. The soil needs to be carefully prepared and the seeds sown somewhat systematically and then when they begin to grow they need individual attention.

In evangelism we are asked to sow seeds and not only should we take care in our sowing but be realistic in our expectations. I only actually grew about eight cabbages out of the dozens of seeds which were planted, but we must not lose heart. Jesus warned us that seed sowing would be a laborious task. Are we prepared to pay the price or are we too easily discouraged by the lack of instant results?

Imagine a sower going out to sow. As he sowed, some seeds fell on the edge of the path, and the birds came and ate them up. Others fell on patches of rock where they found little soil and sprang up straight away, because there was no depth of earth; but as soon as the sun came up they were scorched and, not having any roots, they withered away. Others fell among thorns, and the thorns grew up and choked them. Others fell on rich soil and produced their crop, some a hundredfold, some sixty, some thirty. (Matt. 13:4–8)

Our seed sowing may consist of just giving people food for thought, but we can take consolation from Mark 4:26–8: 'A man throws seed on the land. Night and day, while he sleeps, when he is awake, the seed is sprouting and growing; how, he does not know.'

So one's seed sowing with people is very important especially when they are often being bombarded with every current popular philosophy or receiving their morality from the American soap operas. As Christians we have an important duty, to say to people 'there is another way'.

HARVESTING AND REAPING

As we evangelise we constantly need to rely upon the Holy Spirit by continually opening our lives to him, then we will be directed to the places where there is a rich harvest to be reaped. At various stages during his missionary journeys, St Paul seems to have been directly guided by the Lord. In the Acts of the Apostles it is reported that the Holy Spirit told them not to preach the word in Asia and that the Spirit of Jesus would not allow them to cross into Bithynia (Acts 16:6–8).

A friend of ours is a parish priest in the North East and he told us that each day during his prayer time, he asks the Lord which people he should visit and then he goes out under the guidance of the Holy Spirit. Over the years this type of 'inspirational' visiting has borne much fruit, but it has also demanded a great deal of trust because some of the homes where the priest was led seemed most unlikely places to visit at the time.

When we harvest, as it says in the Scriptures, we often reap the rewards of other people's labours. I was reminded of this a few years ago when we were working in a parish just outside Durham. On the third day of our mission week, I chatted to Sharon, a young mum who told me that she had finally come to a stage where she was being asked to say 'yes' to the Lord and surrender her life into his hands. I arranged to visit her home so that we could discuss this further and it was a great joy for me to help Sharon respond to the Lord, by leading her in a prayer of commitment. However I realised that I was just fortunate to be in the right place at the right time and that Sharon had only been able to arrive at that stage because of the efforts of the parish priest and some of the parishioners over a long period of time.

Harvesting is obviously very exciting and it is always a great honour to be used by the Lord in this way but we must always remember that it is all his work and that we can claim nothing for ourselves. St Paul seemed to have got this in the right perspective when he told the Corinthians: 'I did the planting, Apollos did the watering, but God made things grow. Neither the planter nor the waterer matters: only God, who makes things grow' (1 Cor. 3:6–7).

STREET WITNESS

In my own life I am very much a creature of habit; for instance I have a particular place in my home where I pray and in the parish we are very fortunate to have a beautiful oratory which is so conducive to personal prayer. However I think that there can be a temptation for all of us to keep Christ firmly locked up in church.

Recently whilst reading through the Gospels I was struck by how Jesus not only taught in the synagogues but also out in the open air, often addressing very different audiences. The powerful message of the Beatitudes was for instance delivered out in the open and it was from a boat that Jesus spoke in parables to a crowd gathered by the lake-side. This pattern obviously continued in the early church because by the time Paul reached Athens his evangelism seemed to have two major thrusts. 'In the synagogue he held debates with the Jews and the God-fearing, but in the market place he had debates every day with anyone who would face him' (Acts 17:17).

Today we must also reach out to those around us who desperately need to hear the Good News but who almost certainly will not come to church. We must move out in the power of the Holy Spirit from the meeting place into the market place. There is a part of me which is always uncomfortable with this idea and yet on the other hand I see it as vital, never easy but vital. Perhaps I am continually aware of the many people who are searching for something deeper in their lives because at the age of sixteen I was proselytised by an eastern religious sect in Leeds city centre.

Many people criticise street witness and say that it is undignified and trivialises God or that it is like casting pearls before swine. Obviously we need to be sensitive but I don't think that God is easily trivialised and perhaps we equally do him a disservice by only expecting him to act when we are in church. After all Jesus moved freely about the streets of Galilee meeting people, sharing with them and healing them. As regards casting pearls before swine, this is something which I periodically struggle with and never really come up with any satisfactory answers but what I can say is that the advantages of street witnessing far outweigh the disadvantages.

In the course of evangelism training we have frequently worked with a young people's prayer group in St Albans. Over two years ago in prayer I really felt convinced that the Lord was asking them to step out in faith onto the streets of the city. We spent almost a year praying and discerning this and then we began to do some preparation work and training.

Their evangelism team falls into four main sections. The music group are very lively and because they go out complete with drums, keyboard, amplified guitars and a powerful sound system they soon attract attention particularly from young people.

The music is interspersed with testimonies and drama. Some of the young people have very powerful testimonies about how the Lord has healed them from drug addiction or prostitution or simply about how they have found a positive direction for their lives. These testimonies are always kept short and free from religious jargon and surprisingly large numbers of people are prepared to stop their shopping and listen.

The drama group dressed in their distinctive white boiler suits also quickly attracts a crowd and although some of their sketches are fairly light-hearted, they nonetheless convey important messages about the meaning of life, sin, materialism and so on.

During all this, small groups of people mingle with the crowd talking and sharing their testimony and the gospel message, praying with people and handing out invitations to the prayer group.

One vital section of the team never actually ventures out onto the street, they remain in the church hall praying and interceding during the time that the outreach is taking place. Prayer support is absolutely essential and I would never take a team onto the streets if there wasn't a group backing us up in prayer.

During the past year we have gone out into the main shopping centre once each month, usually on Saturday afternoons, and the results have been very encouraging. Literally, dozens of new people whom we met in the street have attended the Wednesday evening prayer group and many of these have been individually 'discipled' by prayer group members and are now leading fulfilling Christian lives.

On our very first outreach we met a girl called Nicki who has since become a Christian and a regular member of the group. And it is because of people like her that I am convinced of the effectiveness and power of street witnessing.

Nicki's parents were divorced when she was seven years old and illogically blaming herself she thought that she had done something terrible to make this happen. Although her father lived nearby, he never came to visit and Nicki felt very rejected by him. In fact as a young girl she says that she seemed to live in a shell in order to protect herself from further rejection.

In her early teens she got involved with a gang of teenagers who were always in trouble with the police but Nicki eventually broke away from them, when they began to experiment with drugs. Consequently, she completely cut herself off from the world and led a very lonely, boring life, mainly lazing around the house and watching television. Things were on a downward spiral and at the age of seventeen due to intense loneliness, isolation and a poor self image, Nicki had come to the desperate conclusion that she would be better off dead.

Her mind was actually contemplating suicide when she met us in the shopping centre and immediately her attention was drawn towards the young people who looked so alive and happy. As she stopped and listened for a while, a girl from the group was giving her testimony about how Jesus had healed her from drug addiction and how she believed that he would help anyone if they would just give him a chance. Nicki says: 'For the first time in my life someone had given me hope. Maybe Jesus could help me.' She then took the brave step of agreeing to go along to the prayer group and gradually she has received much healing and put her life totally into the hands of the Lord. She is now able to say, almost a year later, 'I'm beginning to really like myself now, and suicide is the furthest thing from my mind. Jesus has shown me how good life can be and now I want to live it.'

Practicalities of street witness

1. Only go out street witnessing in response to the Lord. It is therefore important to spend time interceding for your local area and asking the Lord if he wants you to go out. I am convinced that prayer is the keystone of successful street witness, so we should heed St Paul's advice and 'pray at all times'.

2. Be clear about your aims. Since in St Albans, the group was mainly composed of young people, we were particularly trying to reach out to other

young people in the city. Some groups may just feel called to take a Christian presence onto the streets and proclaim from the 'housetops' that Jesus is Lord (Luke 12:3). Others may want to invite people to a Christian event in which case it is good to have literature or invitation cards to distribute.

3. Get police and/or council permission. The exact nature of this varies from one part of the country to another and as some local authorities actually forbid 'religious' demonstrations you will need to be very clear about the nature and intention of the witness.

4. An occasional witness can be done rather informally but if your group feels called to go out regularly it would be advisable to get some training in practical skills for street evangelism.

5. A great deal of thought needs to be put into the 'content' of the witness so that it meets people where they are; so singing Victorian hymns and reading from the Authorised Version of the Bible will not attract the attention of the majority of people. We have found testimonies to be very powerful especially if they are kept short and simple and delivered with conviction. Always be prepared to share aspects of the gospel message and pray with people.

DOOR-TO-DOOR EVANGELISM

It is probably evident from my frequent references that my community invests a lot of time in door-to-door evangelism. Usually this takes place within the context of a parish mission, where we would visit the regular church members, mainly trying to encourage them in their faith, and we would also visit lapsed members and any other people who have ever had any connections, however tenuous, with the church. Prior to our visits we usually send out a letter informing people that we are visiting in the area and therefore they are to some extent expecting us.

This style of systematic, targeted visiting is very effective and recently we have been involved in training people as parish evangelists, so that they can develop a system of visitation which is tailor-made to their particular situations. On several occasions we have visited all the homes in an area using cold-call methods (arriving unannounced to anonymous households) but this is very labour intensive, less productive, and perhaps only really successful if it is part of a church's long-term vision and strategy.

Again, I am aware that many people have reservations about door-to-door evangelism and liken it to the job of a door-to-door salesman or feel that it reduces Christianity to a level held by religious sects, who are noted for their house-to-house visitation and are seen by many people to be a complete nuisance. As always we need to be sensitive to people and adopt techniques which respect their privacy and freedom and are not pushy or aggressive.

I have literally visited thousands of homes throughout the UK and I can say from experience that it is absolutely essential that we take the Church out to where people are. Far from being hostile, the majority of people are welcoming and are perhaps able to be more receptive to the message in the comfort and security of their home.

I could give dozens of examples which convey the

importance of door-to-door evangelism but perhaps the following one is the most moving.

Almost four years ago, Sr Agnes from our community visited Wacia and Alan at home in Leicestershire. Since then they have become very close friends; however at the time Wacia was a lapsed Catholic and Alan who was suffering from a severe cancer, affecting many parts of his body, had no particular religious conviction. They both now regard the visit as the start of something very precious for the whole family.

Wacia recently told me that they can still clearly recall Sr Agnes sitting in their lounge, sharing about God's deep and personal love for them. They were greatly inspired by her faith and by the way that she spoke with such conviction and sincerity, but unquestionably, the high point of the whole visit was when Agnes asked them very gently if she could pray with them. Apparently nobody had ever done that before and initially Wacia was worried about Alan's reaction so she glanced at him before agreeing. Although they can't remember the exact details of the prayer, they know that it left them with a profound sense of peace and joy and touched them very deeply.

After the visit they both felt a little shell-shocked and they stood in silence for a few minutes hugging each other, then Alan asked, 'What do you think?' to which Wacia immediately replied, 'I think that we should try and find God again'. Unfortunately the following week Alan was admitted to the Royal Marsden Hospital and had to undergo extensive surgery for the rapidly advancing cancer. As the weeks passed by they gradually realised that God had already come to them, but they had to make a conscious decision to put their lives into his hands. This they did and they began to get involved in the life of their thriving parish community. Last Easter it was a great joy to see Alan formally welcomed into the Catholic Church, the strength of his new-found faith now being such an inspiration to many of the parishioners. Recently Alan has again been critically ill but he says cheerfully: 'The first time I faced death without God but now I can live forever.'

Practicalities of door-to-door evangelism

1. Be clear about your aims and visit areas systematically, privately taking note of where you have been so that visits are not duplicated.

2. In order to make the visits personal, it is advisable where possible to know the names of the people in the household. Obviously the parish records will be invaluable but further details can be easily obtained from the electoral register.

3. Always visit in twos because this was how Jesus sent his disciples out.

4. As in all evangelism the spiritual preparation is vital, so as you arrive outside the home pray for each member of the family that you will be given opportunities to share with them.

5. You go out in the name of the Lord so approach each door with confidence. Avoid looking too official, never carry a large Bible or clipboard because these can easily become barriers to communication.

6. Be aware of your body language, relax your

face and appear pleasant and smiling but without wearing an unctuous expression! Also be attentive to their body language, it is so easy in our enthusiasm or tiredness to overlook the signs that are being displayed and we can end up either arousing hostility or killing receptivity.

7. In order to avoid misunderstanding it is very important on the doorstep clearly to identify yourselves, and you should also carry some means of identification. In visiting it is practical to develop a basic formula which confirms the name of the person who has opened the door; this helps you to introduce yourself and your church and explains why you are visiting. Following a favourable introduction, always ask to enter the home.

8. Once inside the home, you should meet the situation as naturally and spontaneously as possible and the following may be useful as a rough guideline.

(a) Talk about their secular life and make them feel at ease.

(b) If appropriate ask them about their church background. This simply tries to move the conversation towards more spiritual things.

(c) Try to meet people where they are and gear the situation to their needs.

(d) Look for an opportunity to share some aspect of your faith story/testimony.

(e) Then move the conversation to the 'objective' gospel and share aspects of the Good News message.

(f) Offer to pray with them and generally invite them to the church or to meet a small group and if necessary arrange a time for another visit.

(g) Do not overstay your welcome!

8

The Vital Component

Lest after preaching to others I myself should be
disqualified.   (1 Cor. 9:27 RSV)

In an attempt to make myself a quick cup of coffee
recently, I switched on the kettle and went into the
lounge to do some work, which was interrupted by
a lengthy telephone call. As I resumed my reading,
I began to realise that there was rather a pungent
smell emanating from the kitchen and upon investi-
gation I was greeted by a piercing bang as the
element in the kettle blew! I realised that in my
haste I had forgotten actually to fill the kettle and
the small amount of water which had been in the
bottom had quickly evaporated.

On reflection, I think that this domestic incident
can speak to us profoundly about our spiritual lives.
Throughout the Old Testament there are references
to the life-giving properties of water, a theme which
would have been particularly powerful in the arid
climate of Palestine, but in John's Gospel, Jesus on
the Feast of Tabernacles actually says: 'If any man
is thirsty let him come to me! Let the man come and
drink who believes in me' (John 7:37–8). Jesus was
the fulfilment of all that they had hoped for and it

is in him that the believer finds strength but he was also making reference to the Holy Spirit who would succeed him.

No doubt there will be times when all of us feel rather like my kettle, with very little water in it, producing a lot of steam for a short time and then eventually going 'bang' and falling apart. That is why it is essential that we allow ourselves to be constantly refreshed by the living water of the Lord and filled with his Holy Spirit. Apparently someone asked Billy Graham, 'Why are you always praying to be filled with the Holy Spirit?' He replied with a broad grin, 'I need to because I leak!'

A couple of years ago I was speaking at a conference near Sheffield where many of the people attending were involved in leadership and ministry. As I got up to speak on the first day with the security of my well prepared talk in front of me, I felt that the Lord was saying something like: 'My people are tired, they are dried up, they are wilting . . .' In obedience to this word I had to step out in faith and deviate from my prepared material on 'the call to evangelise'. So I shared the word from the Lord and also tried to speak further into their situation. Afterwards several people told me how they had come to the conference feeling really 'burnt out' and not therefore able to be open to the concept of evangelism but during the talk they had felt the Lord refreshing, renewing and empowering them.

Clearly it is very important for each one of us to be continually growing in the Lord through prayer, and yet paradoxically in our busy action orientated lives, prayer is often the first thing to be neglected. I once heard a wise preacher say: 'If you are too busy to pray, you are too busy.' This is very sound advice and I have found that when I do set aside generous amounts of time for personal prayer often I am able to achieve far more than if I was operating in my own strength.

This is especially true in evangelism, which by its very nature usually demands action. However, there is a real temptation for us to become task and achievement orientated, rather than to be Spirit led. The end result will be that we quickly get burnt out and perhaps St Paul recognised this when he was spelling out the hardships and discipline of the apostolic life. He was aware that whilst being absolutely intent on the task of preaching and proclaiming the gospel, he also had a personal responsibility to ensure that he was growing in holiness. As he told the Corinthians: 'I treat my body hard and make it obey me, for having been an announcer myself, I should not want to be disqualified' (1 Cor. 9:27).

In order to avoid repetition, up to this point in the book, I have said very little about prayer but in leaving it until this final chapter, I hope to emphasise its importance as the vital component in evangelism.

In my community over the past few years we have come to see very clearly that prayer and contemplation are essential to evangelism and in response we have established a small house of intercession where members of the community can go for a concentrated time of prayer, reflection and intercession.

There are three types of prayer which I think are particularly important in evangelism: praise, intercession and spiritual warfare, and I want now to examine each of these and give some practical hints.

Personally, I am fairly organised and structured in my prayer life and I particularly enjoy praying the 'Prayer of the Church'. So many of the Psalms are such beautiful expressions of praise to God and many of them would of course have been familiar to Jesus. In fact Jewish spirituality is predominantly one of praise and giving glory to God, which they regard as a sacred duty so praise is not just an expression of their happiness but of their faith.

Faith is more than just an assent to doctrinal truths. It is to do with our lived experience and awareness of Jesus. As we go out desiring to share the Good News with others, we need to step out in faith confident that the Lord is with us. Praise then enables us to keep our eyes fixed on him, rather than focusing upon our fear, weakness or inadequacy. We can draw great strength here from many of the Psalms which assure us of the Lord's guidance and protection. Psalm 56 for instance encourages us to rely on God: 'This I know: that God is on my side. In God whose word I praise, in Yahweh, whose word I praise, in God I put my trust, fearing nothing; what can man do to me?' (Ps. 56:10–11)

When we praise God the focus is removed from ourselves and we give him the glory. This is especially important in evangelism where we can subconsciously fall into the trap of self-glorification. Through praise a channel is opened and the Holy Spirit can begin to act powerfully, then we are no longer worshipping in the flesh and trying to get to God in our own strength but we are worshipping in the Spirit and allowing the Holy Spirit who is within our hearts to manifest himself to us. Therefore praise opens up our spiritual 'senses' and we begin to see the things that the Lord wants us to see and hear the things that he wants us to hear.

I can recall many instances when this has actually happened. For example during a healing service a few years ago, a man came forward for prayer and asked me to pray for his family situation. I had been quietly praising God for most of the evening and as I closed my eyes to pray, I saw a vivid picture of a gun and while wrestling with this image and trying to push it aside I said a rather superficial prayer but I knew that I couldn't leave it there. I was afraid that the man might think that I was some sort of clairvoyant and so I carefully explained to him that the Holy Spirit can speak to us in pictures and then I asked him rather timidly if the gun meant anything to him. Immediately his whole body tensed and his face went bright red, and then he told me that his brother who had been in the army had recently been shot dead in Northern Ireland. He stated that the reason he was praying for his family was that he was particularly angry and bitter about the death and this was causing a rift in the family. That evening we were able to pray for healing, firstly for forgiveness within the man's heart and then for the entire family, and I gave praise to God that I had been able to respond to the promptings of his Holy Spirit.

On many occasions evangelism can be a difficult and onerous task and as we have already seen it is very easy to become discouraged but praise helps us to persevere by reminding us that it is all the Lord's work. I was recently away on retreat, where a Jesuit priest told me, 'When the out-look is bad concentrate on the up-look!' I have found this very encouraging particularly in situations which from my viewpoint seem hopeless or impossible.

Here I am reminded of Paul and Silas who were stripped, flogged and thrown into prison because of their evangelistic zeal among the Romans but rather than feeling totally deflated and despondent, their reaction to such harsh treatment and adversity was to praise God. This had remarkable results because an earthquake caused the prison doors to fly open and chains to fall from the prisoners but Paul and Silas didn't immediately rush off rejoicing at their freedom, they used the opportunity for further evangelism.

> When the gaoler woke and saw the doors wide open he drew his sword and was about to commit suicide, presuming that the prisoners had escaped. But Paul shouted at the top of his voice, 'Don't do yourself any harm; we are all here.' The gaoler called for lights, then rushed in, threw himself trembling at the feet of Paul and Silas, and escorted them out, saying, 'Sirs, what must I do to be saved?' They told him, 'Become a believer in the Lord Jesus, and you will be saved, and your household too.' (Acts 16:27–32)

So we should be encouraged by their faith and when we feel that things are not going well, rather than becoming disheartened we should really praise God.

Practical suggestions

1. Spend at least 5 minutes per day praising God for who he is and what he has done.

2. Before embarking upon any evangelistic outreach, spend a good amount of time praising God.

3. When you have had an opportunity to witness to someone always remember to give God the glory.

4. When things have gone wrong or you feel discouraged, rather than worrying or becoming unduly introspective, give praise to God.

5. Regularly meditate upon and pray the Psalms.

INTERCESSION

For many years I had reduced the powerful prayer of intercession down to my simply asking God to bless things! But last summer, Fr Michael Simpson SJ led our community retreat and we were all given great insights into intercession and why it is so vital in evangelism. He told us that intercession is 'to bear the burden of God for our world'. When we look at the world we see so much that is unholy, so many people whose lives are broken and torn apart by the effects of sin and naturally we are concerned and want to help bring about the reality of God's Kingdom here on earth. This is ultimately why we evangelise. However if from our human perspective so much of what we see around us looks grim, how much more this must offend God, the Creator of all things. He longs for his people to turn to him and receive his transforming love. Through intercession we identify with the poor, the broken, the sinner and then we have to be the presence of Christ for them which brings healing and life. In our hearts the pain, darkness and emptiness of this world encounters the life, death and resurrection of Jesus our Saviour.

The underlying purpose of intercession is indeed very deep because we are not just placing our own needs and concerns before God, although obviously this is important, but we are opening up our hearts so that we can be directed by the Lord, and pray for what he would have us pray for.

Last summer during the Southampton Charismatic Conference, a large group of us went out into the city to do a street witness. We left behind an intercessory group of about forty people. During their time of very deep prayer, one lady had a picture in her mind of us out on the street and of a young man almost missing our actual street witness, so they interceded deeply for that person. When we all gathered together at the end of the afternoon one couple arrived back a little late and shared that as they were leaving a young man had come running up to them and asked what all the excitement was about. They had been able briefly to share with him and they invited him back to our service in the evening. He not only came that night but also went along on several occasions to a young people's Christian group in the city. I am sure that the young man never realised that earlier in the day at least forty people had been specifically praying for him!

If we seriously desire to evangelise, we should earnestly pray daily to be led by the Lord to those with whom he wants us to share. In some cases these may appear to be the most unlikely people but through intercession we are able to be directed by God according to his purposes and then we are not limited by our own human assessments of situations or people.

When planning and organising events there is a

tendency to ask God to bless our ideas and plans rather than to intercede and seek his will. I learnt this lesson the hard way a few years ago when we were leading an ecumenical day of renewal in London. In order to encourage people we invited anyone who wished, to come forward and share how God was working in their lives. As I glanced down the central isle of the packed church, I noticed an incredibly eccentric-looking young man making his way towards the front. In a panic I and the other leaders began to pray silently but my faith only stretched as far as saying, 'Lord, send somebody sensible quickly!' Unfortunately the young man had arrived and taken hold of the microphone. I braced myself and even wondered whether I should subtly move forward and hijack him to save everyone's embarrassment, but it was too late. He began to share how for most of his life he had been a misfit and a failure but how his faith had gradually enabled him to see how precious he is in God's eyes. Then he said to the packed congregation, 'If there is anyone out there who doubts God's love just ask him right now to reveal himself to you in a deeper way because he has changed my life and can also change yours.'

This was undoubtedly a situation where the Lord wanted to speak to his people, and if we as the leaders and organisers of the day had followed our logical human inclinations then most certainly we would have blocked this powerful message.

Practical suggestions

1. In intercession we pray according to God's desires, not our own natural inclinations; therefore

93

we begin by praying in faith for the energy and guidance of the Holy Spirit.

2. We must then surrender our desires and concerns and ask God to place his burden for prayer in our hearts.

3. If necessary wait in silence or in an attitude of expectancy for the prompting of the Holy Spirit. He will reveal those people or situations that we should pray for.

4. Hold the people/situations in our hearts before the Lord that his will might be done.

5. Always have a back-up team of intercessors during any phase of active evangelisation. For instance during our parish missions we invite parishioners to intercede before the Blessed Sacrament during the time when the team are out visiting.

SPIRITUAL WARFARE

To some people 'warfare' language may sound rather strange but to me spiritual warfare is just a rather specific type of intercessory prayer and one which is vital in evangelism. St Paul clearly warned the Ephesians to grow strong in the Lord in order to be able to resist the devil's tactics: 'For it is not against human enemies that we have to struggle, but against the Sovereignties and the Powers who originate the darkness in this world, the spiritual army of evil in the heavens' (Eph. 6:12).

There seem to be two rather extreme approaches to spiritual warfare. On the one hand there are those Christians who have ceased to believe in the Devil or have merely reduced him to some sort of vague negative force. They therefore don't see the need to engage in any type of warfare. However if you don't recognise that there is a battle to be fought, you are definitely on the losing side. At the other extreme there are those people who are unhealthily obsessed with demonic activity and are ready to blame Satan for every misfortune which besets them, from getting caught in a shower of rain, to being late for church.

In evangelism we are taking the Kingdom of Light out into a darkened world and we therefore need to engage in spiritual warfare. First of all we should take the authority of Christ and ask him to protect us against any influence of the powers of evil and a good way of doing this is to clothe ourselves with the spiritual armour as set out in Ephesians 6:14–18.

So stand your ground, with truth buckled round your waist, and integrity for a breastplate, wearing for shoes on your feet the eagerness to spread the gospel of peace and always carrying the shield of faith so that you can use it to put out the burning arrows of the evil one. And then you must accept salvation from God to be your helmet and receive the word of God from the Spirit to use as a sword.

Secondly, we need to pray that the strongholds of Satan may be broken. This might refer to the influence of evil on people's lives or to the evil surrounding particular places and so before engaging in a street witness, it is good to visit the proposed venue prior to the outreach and pray there, claiming the ground for the Lord.

Almost three years ago as part of an evangelisation training day in London, we did a street witness one Saturday in the precinct which is almost in the centre of Portobello Road Market. As we marched through the market area, I noticed that some of the stalls were selling Tarot cards and other objects associated with the occult and other stalls were blatantly pornographic. Later on we met some people who were promoting 'new age religion' and offering generous discounts on a book about astral-planing! At one point we were also interrupted by a group of Hells Angels. Understandably that afternoon, there was a very heavy atmosphere pervading the whole area and at one stage we actually stopped the outreach in order to pray for the area and the people, after which there was more of a spirit of receptivity.

Warfare prayer is powerful because we are not relying upon our own strength which would be useless in the spiritual battle, but we are confidently attacking those things in the spiritual realm which seek to prevent us in our duty of proclaiming the Good News.

> We live in the flesh, of course, but the muscles that we fight with are not flesh. Our war is not fought with weapons of flesh, yet they are strong enough, in God's cause, to demolish fortresses. We demolish sophistries, and the arrogance that tries to resist the knowledge of God.
>
> (2 Cor. 10:3–5)

Practical suggestions

1. Ensure that your Christian life is lived in the light and grounded on the truth of Jesus Christ who came to 'destroy the devil's work' (1 John 3:8).
2. Remain faithful to daily prayer, repentance

and frequent reception of the sacraments, so that the devil doesn't get a foothold.

3. Do not be afraid or discouraged, but remember we are on the winning side and we fight from a position of strength. In the end the Kingdom of God will manifest itself in all power. The victory is assured.

4. Pray daily for 'protection' and when involved in any evangelistic events, pray 'strategically' with a plan and purpose against opposition from evil spirits.

5. Keep things in perspective and put your focus primarily on God's work, so do not over-emphasise spiritual warfare. 'Yet do not rejoice that the spirits submit to you; rejoice rather that your names are written in heaven' (Luke 10:20).

We simply cannot underestimate the importance of prayer. It is indeed the vital component and should underpin all that we do in evangelism, otherwise we will be guilty of building a house upon sand. Prayer can be hard work but if we are really serious, we must persevere and remain steadfast even if things seem difficult or unfulfilling, and additionally we should also be prepared to undertake fasting for specific intentions. After all, this is what Jesus asked his disciples to do.

I hope that this book will have been helpful and encouraging but undoubtedly the best way actually to learn about evangelism is by doing it. Ultimately there are no experts, but we all have an important part to play in this essential ministry. We must simply act in obedience to the Lord's call by doing what we can and then allowing him to do the rest, recognising that at the end of the day it is the Holy Spirit who is the Evangeliser. The following quote which I once read adequately sums up much of what I have been trying to convey:

Evangelism is one beggar showing another beggar where to find the bread of life.